THE COMMON PHILOSOPHY

The Common Philosophy

by

FORREST H. PETERSON

Philosophy Dept., Southern Connecticut
State College, New Haven, Conn.

PHILOSOPHICAL LIBRARY
New York

CONTENTS

Preface

FOR CENTURIES PHILOSOPHY has been regarded as one of the most penetrating of all intellectual disciplines. Art is an example of human self-transcendence by which one expresses himself through his power of creativity. But the study of philosophy is an attempt to go beyond one's immediate self-translation and to achieve some description of the *Being* of all being —a description which is itself final. Philosophy is that intellectual venture by which man attempts to overcome the world; to become one with it in an active conscious experience.

Throughout the many centuries of this quest for ontological experience, man has, however, managed to remove himself from the main course of inquiry. The reason for this is that man contains a baffling mystery within himself which cannot be understood in terms of ordinary ways of knowing. This is the mystery of his own psychic consciousness; and even more directly, his own core of existence. Accordingly, philosophy has sometimes become an analytic isolation of ideas, or in other instances, a loose pattern of generalizing concepts. But while philosophy has been allowed to veer in numerous directions, there is always some persistent call within man for self-representation; for expressing the reality which is mankind on some new scale which more vividly conveys his true reality. In other words, man calls upon philosophy to become common;

to be that instrument of self-identification which he so urgently feels, and needs.

This identification is not easily accomplished. At best, philosophy can only point the way to man's self-knowledge. One reason for the incredibly slow progress which modern man seems to be making in this direction is that he is never able to separate that which is himself from that which is the condition of his existence. That which is the-world-in-man and that which is man-in-the-world are bound together in individual man's existential consciousness. Accordingly, that which is the true spirituality in man does not know itself directly. Its actions toward self-discovery invariably tend toward achieving some outward means of self-identification. Science and art are free from this difficulty because in these cases it is not the identity of the person which is important, but that which is outwardly disclosed. The social disciplines are encumbered with this problem, but they are able to escape much of it by utilizing collective concepts, such as the "group," or the "nation," or the "masses." In philosophy there is also an effort to encounter one's markings by use of such terms as *realism, positivism, naturalism,* or *pragmatism*—each supposedly having its own characteristic virtues. Meanwhile, despite the progress which may be made in a more thorough understanding of collective realities, man as a single being becomes more and more aware of his own abject isolation. Man's case is not that of mere being, but of the need of being. It is that unfathomable mystery of an ontological need which only man himself can know himself as knowing.

ACKNOWLEDGMENT

PRODUCING A MANUSCRIPT for publication is a long and sometimes arduous task. From the moment of initial inspiration to the writing of the closing paragraph an intense and painstaking effort is required to make a vast assortment of ideas cohere and achieve their fullness of meaning. While the writer's task is that of producing and organizing the manuscript material, there is also a need for stylistic criticism for the effective flow of ideas. For her editorial assistance in the preparation of this manuscript, the writer is especially indebted to Mrs. Sylvia Hemstead, Professor of English, Southern Connecticut State College.

The author acknowledges with thanks the permission of the following publishers to quote from their copyrighted works:

The Beacon Press: John Dewey, *Reconstruction in Philosophy;*

Farrar, Straus & Giroux, Inc.: Karl Jaspers, *Reason and Existenz;*

Harper & Brothers, Publishers: Pierre Teilhard de Chardin, *The Phenomenon of Man,* translated by Bernard Wall, copyright, 1955 by Editions du Seuil; copyright © 1959 in the English translation by Wm. Collins & Co. Ltd., London and Harper & Row, Publishers, New York. Used by permission of Harper & Row, Publishers, Inc.;

The Harvill Press Ltd.: Gabriel Marcel, *The Philosophy of Existentialism;*

The Macmillan Company: Ernst Nagel, *Logic Without Metaphysics;*

University of Chicago Press: Paul Tillich, *Systematic Theology,* Vol. II;

Yale University Press, Ernst Cassirer: *The Logic of the Humanities,* translated by Charles Smith Howe.

F.H.P.

THE COMMON PHILOSOPHY

CHAPTER I

The Call for Philosophy

THE PRESENT WORLD POPULATION numbers in the billions. This is humanity multiplying endlessly and stretching as a vast membrane over the whole earth. From the zero meridian east and west, and from polar to equatorial regions, the human family spreads itself relentlessly into every area where life can be sustained. But while the life process itself is one of endless innovation and new organic detail, two facts about human nature stand out. One is that, despite an almost incredible diversity in natural environments, human nature sustains an equally incredible uniformity in performance. Once the barriers of language differences are overcome, there is a remarkable facility for communicating ideas. The second fact is another instance of unity-in-difference. Although there is an apparently endless process of new genetic enumeration, man's existential reality as person is steadily maintained in each new, unique being. There is no evidence of species degradation —of a decline to a sub-human level of existence.

To say that something is a *person* is to convey a certain configuration of meaning. The terms *individual, organic unity, rational being, mind-body composite* all point in some general way to that kind of natural system in which there is engendered *personality,* but no one of these terms carries within its meaning that which illumines the concept of person in all its fullness of being. The term *human* refers in its derivation to *humus*, to man's body being drawn from the soil. But while man's being is undeniably sustained by minerals taken from the earth, human protoplasm does not occur through any chance mixing of elements. Protoplasm itself, wherever it is found, is a great step forward in the natural process because it is an ignition of being on the level of organic synthesis. Random particles of matter, accidentally composed, do not by themselves emerge as conscious and knowing life. It is in living protoplasm itself that organic "complexification" achieves the peak of self-expression—an inner radiance of being which is personality. But because it is not reducible to any biological category, because personalism or personality involves a performance leap far beyond any routine biological phenomenon, there are no access routes by which it can be directly known.

It is here that scientific explanation comes to a dead stop. Scientific knowing is essentially reductive. It breaks apart that which is given as a body of sense data and converts it into a set of intelligible regularities. But life is the work of synthesis on a number of strata levels of elaboration. The reductive method of science contains no intrinsic reverse order within itself. The scientist who reconstructs his data in an attempt to arrive at a new level of synthesis does so at the risk of a loss of quantitative accuracy. The larger configurations of meanings which appear preclude any exact knowing in terms of the meanings of parts. The meaning of a part is possible because a part is itself contained in a higher order of generalization, and the symbol which is attached to it contains something of its intrinsic reference to the higher order. But human personality is not a *part* of anything; it is itself a whole. There is no concrete universal within man's perceptive grasp to which human personality can relate. The term *individual* is a biological category which applies equally well in all levels of organic elaboration. *Person,* however, is an exclusively human quality. It is an apparition of *being,* and as such it is something which can only be transcendentally, but never empirically, defined. A fragmented humanity would not be a humanity at all. Human nature is essentially gravitational. It survives only through coexistence and through involving itself in a continuous throb of communication and interpersonal exchange. Also, it is the symbol, the instrument of communication which is the clue to the rational nature of man. The symbol has a three-fold function: to designate, to accumulate, and to store meanings attached to human experience. It is the first of these, designation, which marks the immense qualitative difference between animal and human behavior. In substituting the symbol for the thing, the phenomenon, or the relation, man enters into a world which is possible for him alone—transcendence over the limitations of concrete, biologically sensed occurrences. In this new world he is no longer bound by the space and time dimensions of a "happening." It is also by means of symbol that man encounters himself in his act of introreflection. That is, through the use of symbol he creates, but causes what he creates to stand apart from himself as a meaning which is held in arrest. But the symbol is also an instrument of interrelation and extension of additional meanings. Like self-fermenting protein structures which catalyze inner organic processes, sets of symbols are capable of inner interrelations which are themselves provocative of new conceptual content.

Many of the activities carried out through the media of interpersonal exchange do, however, concern the ordinary requirements of biological life and of psychological experience. These do, on this account, tend often to fall into some routine. Even when ordinary human experience is punctuated by one or another kind of induced variation, there comes to be even a routine of punctuation. The coffee break, the weekend visit, the trip to the shore or to the mountains, all come to be

3

standardized ways of relaxation. It is small wonder that adult conversation sometimes becomes dull. Adult play is more competitive than creative, and adult maturation seems to cool much of the thrill of childhood expectation. Accordingly, daily living often turns out to be a daily round of doing the ordinary.

Not all, however, of the fire of mind and heuristic passion is buried under the practical. Technology, commerce and service performing tend to become the kinds of urban routines which make socialized human existence a daily treadmill. But in spite of this there is still time to wonder and to think; and the glory of the human intellect lies in its power of transcendence, in its power to "walk in space"—to encounter existence in its outermost reaches of meaning. It was the power to wonder which first surpassed man's power to understand, and this gave rise to myth, rite and ancient religion. True, these may have been brought forth partly by man's deep longing to be secure, to be at one with all that he encountered in one divine order of real existence. But man's intellect had been for some time stirring him more and more toward a conquest of the world of fact. The development of symbol was on the crest of a long period of evolutionary awakening, and by the use of symbol man's intellect was becoming more and more analytic, and also more inwardly cognizant that mind, like other things about him, had its regularities. What was perhaps the first cosmological idea to implant itself firmly in man's mental apprehension was the difference between order and chaos. Man was coming to recognize the ideality of order, both for the protection by which an ordered life kept a body from harm and for an emerging new form of ideality—that of the tranquility of soul. What gave rise to custom in antiquity was not some chance agreement, some happenstance of fate; but rather that which stabilized the ways in which men lived together. It was *custom* which shaped and gave content to the moral atmosphere in

4

which men moved. This seems to have been prevalent in all the great systems of ethics. Ernst Cassirer wrote:

> In their cosmogonies and moral teachings all great religions have based themselves on this theme. They are unanimous in attributing to the creator a double role and a two-fold task—to be the founder of the astronomical and moral orders and to rescue both from the forces of Chaos. In the Gilgamesh Epic, in the Vedas, in the Egyptian creation story we find the same vision. In the Babylonian creation myth we see Marduk waging battle against shapeless Chaos, against the monstrous Tiamat. Following his victory he erects these eternal monuments of the cosmic and moral orders; he determines the course of the stars, he establishes the signs of the zodiac; he fixes the succession of days, months and years. At the same time he sets limits to human action, limits which cannot be transgressed with impunity.[1]

Cassirer is referring here to the thematic work in man's imagination which constructs an order for the world in line with his inner desires and deeper feelings. Egyptian and Babylonian cultures carried their respective civilizations far through the mastery of mathematics and astronomy. With these intellectual tools they were able to measure in many ways the external world of fact. But they began also to realize that *measure* applies in some ways to man himself. They began to suspect that there were forces in the cosmological order which shaped and conditioned man's own way of life. If their moral constructions took shape as myth, this does not imply that they were given to fantasy rather than to intellectual sincerity and precision. It was by use of myth that they were able to

---

[1] Ernst Cassirer, *The Logic of the Humanities* (New Haven: Yale University Press, 1961), p. 42.

make their moral ideas cohere—to complete by fantasy what they could not complete by fact.

In the philosophy of Greek antiquity the same use of myth is deeply entrenched. The figures of "water" in the writings of Thales and of "fire" in those of Heraclitus may not have referred to these figures as they are encountered in practical experience, but perhaps to some homogeneous fluid out of which all things emerge. In the *Timaeus* of Plato, man's soul is said to be identical with the lower part of the soul of the world. But in this work there occurs also that break in the use of myth which points to the use of a more literal language in philosophy. Plato acknowledged that the description of creation in the *Timaeus* was no more than a "likely account."

The mythical character of the *Republic* ought, of course, be acknowledged. Yet this was not a flagrant, but a guarded, use of the kind of metaphor which Plato employed to draw out the meaning of justice. It is true that, for Plato, the Forms were transcendent entities. They could not be found anywhere and could not be encountered in concrete experience. But for Plato the ideal world was real. The Forms stood above the changing and the contingent. Man's individual body could rot and decay, but the Form—man's existential truth—could never be obliterated. Individual man is born, he can multiply through reproduction, and he must at some time die. But the Form of man is never born, it does not agglomerate, and it does not die. Because as a mode of *being* it supports the world of fact, it can never be erased from it. It survives anything which can happen to man on earth.

The Forms were also a means toward another significant achievement in philosophy. As ideal types these were the instruments by which things could be logically classified. In this way these bore a direct relation to the world of fact. But the Forms were themselves also interrelated. They could be arranged in a hierarchy which had an ascending order of universality. In this way they were also a means toward the ontological unification of the natural world. Plato accomplished two things by this step. One was his affirmation that the *true* is never completely present in a single object of sense. Everything which is given in appearance is marked by limitation, and its participation in the *true,* the *real,* is, therefore, diminutive. In fact, nothing taken in isolation reveals anything of Truth at all. Only by grasping the object in terms of the class, the species in which it falls, does one arrive at any universally valid concepts.

The second thing accomplished by this step was Plato's recognition of *order* as an underlying principle of intelligibility, and presumably then also, of things as they exist. Plato did not raise the epistemological question whether the world presented itself to the mind as essentially ordered in itself or whether it was mind which imposed the order inherent in its own nature upon the world. The important side of Plato's argument did not concern this issue at all; it concerned rather the idea that *chaos* is not something positive in itself—that it is an aberration from that which is positively real. What he accomplished especially well in this regard was to put matter and the Forms in a proper perspective. That is, the two were not taken as necessarily in opposition. Since matter could be *ordered,* it need not be taken as a principle of disaster; a position from which many later religions could have capitalized.

In the metaphysics of Aristotle, philosophy came to have an even more literal bearing on experience. Plato's Forms were lacking in one major respect; they did not give any kind of accounting of the world being continually transformed within itself; they did not make the transition from *being* to *becoming.* For Plato, the Good is a resplendent ideal. As such it is necessarily remote from that which undergoes experience. But for Aristotle *goodness* is something to be achieved. It is something which must be wrought out of the natural processes in existence by a dynamic unfolding of what exists primordially as inner potential. Goodness is something which becomes. Nothing in nature is in a state of complete arrest. Every structure undergoes a cycle of fulfillment of its natural end, and the *goodness* associated with this process consists of the excellence in the way that its function is made complete. For Aristotle, the Good is not some ontological lure standing behind and shaded by the natural order. The Good is in nature itself, in the telic pattern by which it moves toward its moments of completion.

As might be expected under the incisive exposure of more exact and more precise descriptions in natural science, Aristotle's accounting of the physical world came to be regarded as far from adequate. But his metaphysical reduction of living structures to act-potency composites and his fourfold division of causality have stood very well the wear of time and scientific innovation. His categories have remained largely unchallenged. Even his methodological error of assuming that things actually exist in the ways they are grasped in the categories of the mind has not aroused much comment. But what became an issue, and a very grave one for modern philosophy, is the certainty which one could have for existential knowledge. It was in modern philosophy that the whole problem was thrust into a new light and subjected to a more critical assessment of the conditions of knowing.

It was in the works of Descartes that the matter of certainty was first put to a severe test. Aristotle's psychology had never raised the critical issue of what the real juncture between concrete physical impressions and immaterial ideas was. It did not raise the issue of how an essential harmony between the rules of each could be actually supported by evidence. Nor was a serious doubt ever raised about the validity of the universal—the main item in the controversy between Peter Abelard and William of Champeaux in the Middle Ages.

8

But Descartes' speculations were to bear the onus of destructive criticism. His attempts to reduce all human knowledge to simple, clear and distinct ideas was an honest enough attempt to resolve all complex phenomena into knowable units. But while Descartes hoped that this method would also incur the promise of certainty, it turned out, paradoxically, to assure only uncertainty. His clear and distinct idea of man as a knowing subject contained no reference to man as a physical being. Similarly, his clear and distinct idea of man as a *body* did not imply in any way that this body also *thinks*. In the evidence given by mind in its primary unit of intelligibility, mind and body are unalterably opposed. The integrity of mind, of the self which knows and thinks, could be preserved only by isolating the concept of mind from that of matter. Thought and body extension are two separate concepts for which there is no apparent reconciliation. But man is given in appearances as both. Because man is irrevocably tied to the world of sense, his crowning intellectual discipline—philosophy—must give up its hope of encountering what the real truth of existence is. Descartes pushed his speculation so far that, for him, existential knowledge could not be held as certain through the use of the mind's own tools and its own rules. Because of William of Ockham's denial of the reality of universals near the close of Medieval Scholasticism, there was little support for the basic position of the metaphysical universal. Certainty about one's own existential condition could not now be found except by way of a return to faith. Descartes found it necessary to prove that a just and veracious God exists who would not deceive man by creating two different worlds not oriented to each other.

In the *Critique of Pure Reason* Immanuel Kant brought the matter of real knowledge once more into focus. To what extent could existential knowledge be accommodated in any metaphysical system? This was the question to which Kant addressed himself, and toward which solution he made such a long and searching inquiry. But because of his own genius for exposing the problem in all its depth, and also because of his strong grasp of the arguments of Locke and of Hume, he deepened the problem far more than he solved it. The study of metaphysics, in which the principal objective had been the conquest of the noumenal world—the world of Plato's Forms—was now relegated to a critical science. It could only concern itself with the conditions of knowing. It could not aim directly at that body of truth which philosophers had long supposed existed, but which was unreachable.

The deep rift created by Descartes between the worlds of ideality and materiality had now been explored quite completely from within. Like Descartes, Kant also found it necessary to return to a position of faith; faith in the existence of a moral law, faith in the autonomy of man's will, and faith in the existence of God as the Creator of both. Moreover, Kant's antinomies, each one supplying cogent arguments for both rationalist and empiricist positions, left philosophy in a hopeless deadlock from which neither of the opposing sides could rise to a critical superiority. The only way out of the impasse seemed to be a position of "identity-indifference." The old dualism of being and knowing had now to be overcome by a bold stroke of discovering their utter identicalness in a new ontology. Philosophy could handle once more the major questions of ontology by becoming total; by becoming in some way *one* with the world and of history.

The first step appeared to be that of dissolving the content of philosophy into that of its method. Content presupposes an existential world of fact; method presupposes an existential subject. In a radical reconstruction of logic in which fact and method are shown as opposing moments of an Absolute Subject, truth is something which *becomes*. A system of universal logic, a logic of the whole—one which is not private and personal, but cosmic—began to take shape in Fichte's deduction of the Consciousness of the Absolute Ego. Like Kant, Fichte denied that man can have a direct intellectual intuition of any noumenal reality. But from the standpoint of the pure creative activity of the Absolute Ego, intuition is the productive activity of pure Consciousness. In making a distinction between man's ectypal intelligence and the archetypal, creative intelligence of God, Kant was in his own way anticipating the dialectic of universal consciousness which was to originate in Fichte's system and to reach its fruition in Hegel's Logic of the Absolute. If God's way of knowing is identical with His way of creating, then there is in God none of the opposition between the knowing subject and the object which the subject knows. God, as Absolute, is the source, not only of His own truth, but also of man's way of apprehending it. But Fichte did not develop his system any further than the self-positing act of the Ego.

It remained for Hegel to draw out all the implications of the self-positing activity of the Absolute. It seemed to Hegel that Kant's failure to open a path to true knowledge, to accommodate existential fact in a pure science of metaphysics, left but one way open for philosophy; and this was to resolve the whole problem of the opposition between subject and object in a universal, creative Logic. For Hegel the content of philosophy could no longer be seen as a purely formal accounting of reality; as consisting only of the meager kinds of thinking which are brought to bear on man's immediate experience. As Universal Logic, philosophy is constitutive of the entire world process because it is grounded in the reflective-creative activity of the Absolute. Man must now recognize his own subjectivity as caught up in the march of history; as the instrument of the Absolute in its being externalized and emptied into time. Human history is thus conceived by Hegel as the march of God on earth; of God revealing Himself through the process of historical becoming.

The sharp cleft between experience and knowledge is now dissolved. Experience is not seen here as something into which mind places itself. It is Mind's own production, its way of seeing itself doubled. Truth, as Hegel regarded it, emerges out of an unconditioned unity of subject and object. It is the character of the Absolute, but the Absolute is also Spirit, of which Hegel wrote: "It is alone Reality. It is the inner being of the world, that which essentially *is* and is *per se;* it assumes objective determinate form, and enters into relations with itself."[2] It enters into relations with itself through man's productive activity in art, morality, religion, science and philosophy. It is through these that the force of the Universal is asserted and becomes determinate. It is through man's subjective willing that Spirit as objective Right opposes itself to itself and asserts its determinate character in the areas of morality and law. Only through man's transgressions and through Spirit's activity qua universal morality and objective Right in bringing man back out of this unreality does the moral force of law reveal itself as universal consciousness.

Hegel's Logic of the Absolute has many roots. There was, for one thing, Plato's plurality of Forms which no doubt impressed Hegel with the idea of the totality of the world being given in some absolute concept. Then there was Giordano Bruno's postulate concerning the "one and the same scale" of God's creative power descending to the world and man's mind ascending in its knowledge of things. If this could be literally the case, then logic and causality have a common root identity. There was also Spinoza's pantheism; the idea of God revealing Himself to man by externalizing Himself substantially in the

---

2 G. W. F. Hegel, *Phenomenology of Mind*, tr. J. B. Baille (New York: The Macmillan Company, 1931), p. 86.

natural world. Once that Kant had shown in his antinomies the futility of a genuine metaphysical reduction of the world of fact, the way was open for Hegel to assemble his dialectic as a final answer to what had seemed to be a hopeless conflict of transcendental ideas. When subject and object are shown as reciprocating moments of the Absolute, as alternate moments of the Absolute in its acts of introreflection, there would be no polar opposition which could not be resolved.

With the pendulum of speculation reaching such an unprecedented extreme on one side of metaphysical dualism— that of ideality, it was not surprising to note another arc being traced in the direction of materiality. With Marx and Engels, the recognition of historical time as the unconditioned eon of social production was a call to reconstruct philosophy in terms of man's own natural condition and practical concerns. Again there was the raising of an absolute, but this time it was *matter* rather than God as Spirit which was the single sole reality. For the Marxist matter was being-in-itself; the *being* of all being, including human consciousness and also, indirectly, human history. The Marxist dialectic of world materialism lays claim to all of human history and thereby also to the evolutionary destiny of man himself. Man's claim to justice based on an eternal order of right is rejected, as it was by Hegel, and for very much the same reason—there is only the abstract right of historical becoming which can at any moment cancel out any private right of man-in-the-flesh. Hegel took the position of man-in-the-flesh being subject to the severe demands of history as necessary in order that the abstract right implicit in the march of God on earth could become externalized in history. The Marxists, on the other hand, saw rightness as having no original place in the ethical community other than to represent the interests of the most powerful class. For them morality was a spurious delusion invented by religion; and religion was in turn invented by the ruling class in order to govern the minds of the workers by fear. Metaphysical interests fared no better. The Marxists saw these as nothing more than the idle concern of a decadent bourgeois society.

In the wake of such revolutionary appropriation of the subject matter of philosophy, it is not surprising that there is seldom found in contemporary philosophy a real sense of central direction. Because of its highly abstract quality, Hegel's Logic had little appeal for people of average intelligence, and what is really germane in it for present inquiry has been absorbed in a variety of neo-Hegelian systems. The strength of Marxism seems to spring more from a rejection of certain political systems than from any real interest in an ontological accounting of existence. It is more a popular social doctrine than a philosophy. It is something which can be accepted or rejected by use of arguments which never come close to exposing its methodological errors.

What has survived from both systems is the sense of the historical. Once this dimension was added to the sphere of philosophical investigation, it became impossible to discard it thereafter. For it was in philosophy expressed as a social dialectic that man's subjectivity itself began to play an immense role. This is hardly a contemporary development. As far back as the works of St. Augustine, the subjective and the historical in man played a prominent part. There were pronounced traces of the historical element in the social contract theories of Hobbes, Locke and Rousseau; and also in the social positivism of Auguste Comte. But it was primarily in the nineteenth century that the themes of the subjective and the historical became exaggerated. Philosophers are well aware, for example, of the intense self-examination and the searching agony which precedes Kierkegaard's "leap into faith." For Nietzsche the theme is world-recurrence, capturing the eternal in time through man's will-to-power. It was this piece of philosophical dogma which shaped his entire outlook.

The task of carrying out a philosophical resynthesis of history is indeed staggering. There are few philosophers who have the background of historical detail for detecting the underlying movements accounting for the growth and also the decay of whole civilizations. Most historians seem to lack the philosophical acumen to detect those instances in history when man literally acts out a larger than usual role of humanization. Yet this is a task to which philosophy must address itself. It took time to discover that the Logos of the world was not some static, fixed order of being from which the natural world had gone astray. Not until the philosophers' views of history were extended far into the modern period could the philosopher of history discern how social activity is an essential part of the order of the world. Man is himself caught up in an incessant flux of transformation, but in order to form some real concepts of his own nature, he must be able to hold certain elements of natural phenomena in arrest. Plato's Forms, Aristotle's Categories and his fourfold division of causality enabled philosophers to recognize some of the elements of substantiality which underlie a physical order continually falling apart and restructuring itself. But the difficulties involved in achieving a precise assessment of historical man are well known. What has to be dealt with is not a succession of phenomena which can be repeated at will, but rather a human consciousness which is itself evolutionary. It is continuously expressing itself in new and varied dimensions. Furthermore, human consciousness is highly refractory to any analysis of itself; it can never undergo any thorough self-examination at close range. Human events require a distance perspective in time in order to be seen in their proper focus, but this distance perspective entails the risk of a loss of detail and meaning.

Numerous attempts have been made to expose the real facts of consciousness by following the rules of strict empirical analysis. In whatever style of inquiry, the appeal of scientism is indeed strong. The development of an impartial, unprejudiced attitude is certainly commendable for many reasons, but, by maintaining an entirely dispassioned attitude, one is not easily able to assume a critical position of qualitative evaluation. For example, Freud's *id, ego* and *superego* throw a fresh light on both normal and abnormal behavior. By a purely statistical accounting of behavior patterns, Freud concluded that the existence of the superego as an inner "judge" was a plausible hypothesis. But even if the hypothesis is correct, the presence of an internal judge is just one more statistic. The hypothesis says nothing about the universal standards as the means and the primary cause of the superego judging as it does.

Despite the immense range and deep penetration of empirical inquiry, the major questions regarding man's nature go unanswered, and, to a large extent, uninvestigated. The man of science applies his tools of research to what is determinate and submits to quantitative definition. But his own passion for exactness and his dedication to his own chosen goals escape any such instrumentation. That heuristic passion and intellectual appetite involve some form of energy release seems to be a plausible position. But this may be no more than an ordinary release of biological energy. One can raise the question whether the work of consciousness is biological energy coming to focus through some form of structural convergence.

The mystery of consciousness, of its power to convey an awareness of *I,* prevents one from answering this question. Molecular particles cannot be observed, even with the most powerful electron microscopes, for the simple reason that the electron beam from the microscope affects the electron structure of the molecule so that it necessarily disturbs the very object which is to be examined. The analogy is not an exact one, but it shows the main reason for man's failure to understand his own consciousness—the fact that man's only approach to the phenomenon of consciousness is through consciousness itself. Terms which refer properly only to nonconscious activity point only in a very vague way to the content designated. One can speak of consciousness in terms of the energy associated with it, but this does nothing toward discovering its constituent elements.

In spite, however, of being barred from a solution to the nature of consciousness, one can make some progress by using certain salient facts about man in the world. There is, for example, man's uniqueness which consists in part of his being able to relate himself to his environment in a much greater degree than any other living thing. On lower levels of participation, a massive portion of the natural order exists and interacts alongside definite lines of functional stratification. From the very simplest particles to the highly complex human structure, there is an ascending order of physical and biophysical systems operating in interrelations of dependence and support. The stratification exists because particle behavior does not occur in a single homogeneous routine. The atom, for example, has a routine function which is its own. It does not interrupt this internal procedure when it becomes part of a molecular structure. Its capacity for interaction is increased with every increased structural whole in which it becomes a part. That is, large molecular aggregates become what they are because of the capacity of the lesser particles to sustain larger and larger structural units. Similarly, molecules come to belong to large mega-molecular bodies. By an increase in complexity and size, these culminate in the formation of protein structures, virus particles, and, eventually, cells. Each novel emergent in the series is a new synthesis in which energies combine. The cell, however, contains new and novel features which point in some way to the heuristic passions resident in man's behavior as a person. The cell is far more than just another energy bond. It is a system of energy exchange with its

17

own existential media. It must immerse itself in this media in order to satisfy its own special requirements for life.

This is, however, just an elementary manifestation of what the astounding aspects of cellular production and interaction are. From here a new set of terminology is required to convey the phenomena of corpuscular masses expressing themselves in a manner which can be described in no less a manner than as psychic. One can say that there are now new forms of regularity and media of existential interaction, but then one is expressing new phenomena by old terminology. One asks what conveys the principle of life and what symbols set off the living from the nonliving. Protoplasm, phylia, germination— all point to features which belong to life alone. Reproduction, conjugation—these also belong to this line of existents. One can also add the concept of *controlled additivity*. But the really dynamic quality of life—one which dynamically characterizes all living existents—is *orthogenesis*. This is the activity resident within the life impulse extending itself by an immense variety of phyletic structures in which specialized forms of being come to be hardened and permanently expressed existentially.

The concern of philosophy is not, however, just with an accumulation of biological facts. Biology is, of course, a preliminary area of study, since in it, as in biochemistry, one can follow some lineal pattern of structural emergence. But one also hopes to find here some traces of the apparition of consciousness, and from this some of the preliminary forms of intuition and analytic reason. Like the facts of physics, those of biology do incur the possibility of prediction. But consciousness involves more than just reaction to what is copresent with it in the environment. When taken in the total sense of phyletic spiritualization, consciousness includes the continual surge of what is deeply interior in one's psychic being. It is from within that there issues forth a certain spontaneity, a freedom from within which is set against determinateness from without. As a result of this, human behavior is far less predictable than that of species whose behavior patterns have become frozen into a routine of set instinctual responses. In man's case one must reckon with a complex of deep desires, singular motives, and even prejudiced attitudes. Not even man's reason can be counted on as invariably determining or even shaping his conduct. Because of his own peculiar freedom, man is able to shut off, to divert, to stifle the pressure of the logic of his own mind.

The real problem lies in this irregularity in his patterns of thought and action. Freedom and regularity—two recognized and publicly acknowledged *goods in behavior*—are frequently opposed. Neither is completely good in itself nor completely evil. The one is the essential truth of the mind, the other a necessary characteristic of the body. As a result the essential truth of the spiritual composite—man—has always been somewhat obscure. This is a problem which metaphysics tries directly to probe and solve, for it alone makes a distinction between the power of freedom and its use. It alone recognizes that freedom is not a suspension of regularity altogether, but rather that there is another kind of regularity attached to freedom which is nonbiological. Common notions of freedom arise when one senses an absence of physical or biological determinateness. To this absence one assigns some general feeling of value. But it is precisely at this point that common notions of freedom have gone astray. It is at this nexus of the material and the nonmaterial that the sense of *value* originates. Value certainly pertains to structures far lower than man's own level. Even nonconscious things, such as plants, respond to value situations. But the apparition of value in a concept could hardly occur to nonconscious structures. Only through a genuine awareness of self and of that which is other than one's self could this occur, and only through enlarging the notion of consciousness could one be able to see the place which

19

value has in it. For *value* is consciousness asserting itself as spirit. Value is, in effect, "that which will become." Freedom as consciousness is no empty idea. It is the regularity of Spirit acknowledging its independence from matter by opposing itself to it. In orthogenesis, matter is the passive instrument. It submits to the pressures of consciousness as possibility, which matter and material processes are called upon to fulfill. In the ascending order of living structures there are definite instances of phyletic stratification—there is dependence of the higher upon the lower in areas of novelty and freedom, and the growing levels of "complexification," reaching from the simplest to the higher forms of consciousness and reflective activity—all concrete examples of matter submitting at successive levels to higher and higher designs of incorporation. One such example is the human brain. The brain is the material substrate of the mind. It is the material instrument by which the mind works. But it is not mind itself; it does not deploy itself at the reflective process. It is only mind as spirit which operates on this high level of organizational mastery, and, in organizing matter to carry out its necessary neural connections, it diffuses itself.

The diffusion of spirit takes place in individual persons having their own separate consciousness and their own susceptibility to ideas and feelings of value. But this diffusion also leads to a number of problems in collective existence. To what does consciousness, now resident in mankind, point? Naturalist and contemporary humanist philosophers insist that it points toward nothing beyond itself. They would insist that all of the meaning and fullness of consciousness are to be found in human experience. They would insist that nature is just what it is; that its material origin is to be taken for granted, and that any idea of a transcendental order of creativity outside of this material order is meaningless as far as human experience is concerned.

The point which naturalist and humanist philosophers raise might be pertinent were it not that they are often the most vocal in their call for a transcendental order of value. The efforts of naturalist philosophers to discover in nature the necessary antecedents of every idealist expression of man and the efforts of humanist philosophers to delineate human concerns in natural situations are all overt expressions of a commitment to a transcendent order of human spirituality. The very character of philosophy, especially as social theory, presupposes a concern for some adequate collectivist expression, and every move is a step toward rationalizing some transcendent ideal. If this ideal is not itself discoverable in universal consciousness as a transcendent reality, as appealing to all men, then at least it is consciousness in individual man which is pointing to its necessary character.

Each of the specialized areas—the sociological, the economic, the historical, the psychological—furnishes a set of clues which illumine the issue in some way, and each one furnishes the investigator with its own set of data. But in no case do the conclusions drawn reach the precision of anatomical studies. Each carries results which are provisional in that they have to be interpreted in view of a whole area of inquiry which includes all the rest. Contemporary philosophy must also specialize in order to bracket what does not come directly within the purview of other areas of study. The separate areas of specialization continue to show new ways of inquiry, new and refreshing formulations of man's position as a component of the natural order, and of his focus in history. But in bracketing that which does not enter directly into these individual areas of inquiry, some contemporary philosophers have to begin at positions already presupposed in other areas. Naturalism, for example, takes as its starting point man's biological self. It does not find it necessary to inquire into what brought the human species to its present level of performance. It accepts the fact of man's interaction with his physical environment without ever pausing to examine whether there was any enveloping system existing beforehand from which man could emerge. Existentialist philosophers begin at a point which is, evolutionary, much later—not with biological man at all or with man's natural environment, but with man turned inward upon himself to encounter his troublesome subjectivity. Contemporary philosophers seldom go further into the depths of man's being than that which has already been revealed in analytic psychology, no further in comprehending history than do historians who weave their own fabric of the human story; and they leave the analysis of myth, rite and symbol to the specialists of language and symbolic forms.

But why should philosophy go further? What could it possibly hope to achieve which has not been done in other fields of specialization? The call for philosophy comes from the urge among men to secure an ultimate, final reduction of what the real content of existence is. It comes from the heuristic passions which well up within man to know the whole of his being in all its fullness of meaning. It does not ask just what life is, but also, why there is life. Contemporary philosophers, anxious to avoid stirring dead metaphysicians back to life, tend toward narrow forms of specialization. But their own speculative horizons come to be too restrictive to permit a wide perspective. Man is lonely, Sartre concludes, and his loneliness can only invite despair. What makes man that way is that there is no God to whom he can refer his sense of guilt and plead for merciful forgiveness. Accordingly, man is thrown back upon himself to live with his own guilt complexes and with his freedom to incur more of them. Everything is turned upside down. Anxiety turns the daylight of consciousness into the dread of a long night of meaningless existence, and the nighttime of death is the only hope of release. Man must choose—but only because he was born free—and in this way he is condemned. For Sartre, man has nothing to fulfill. But what then does the existentialist do to bring mankind back into the daylight of hope and feeling and to give meaning to existence? Why was it that the maniacal Hitler could do what gifted philosophers often fail to do—give men a living faith in themselves and in their destiny when all hope and faith in the future seem to have vanished? Why does it take a madman to give people a reason for living and a reason for dying? Why does the philosopher, in a quest for the ultimate reality, so often lose his sense of the real in time; and then, because he has lost it, insist that there is nothing discoverable as real anywhere?

The real reason might well be that there are things which block the philosopher's vision as completely as that of anyone else. The "things" are the artifacts—millions of them—mass produced and driving man the producer out of his position as the main social focus. It is not man himself, but what he brings forth—what he produces—which is the bearer of value. The result is that there is a proliferation of new devices which shape and affect man's existence faster than he is able to accustom himself to them. Ernst Cassirer writes:

> Through the use of tools man has made himself supreme over things. But, instead of a state of abundance, this supremacy has become a curse. The technical science which man has invented in order to control the physical world has, in fact, turned against him. It has led, not only to an ever-increasing self-estrangement, but ultimately to a species of self-extinction. The tool, which appeared to be destined for the fulfillment of human needs, on the contrary, has created countless artificial needs. Each elaboration of technology is, and remains a treacherous gift. Hence the yearning for primitive, unbroken, immediate existence repeatedly breaks forth. The more numer-

23

ous the areas of life taken over by technology, the louder the call, "Back to nature." [3]

But is there really any chance of going "back to nature" in man's present state? One of the efforts of technology has been to make man's original condition in nature more and more obscure. One would have to learn something more about man in his prelingual, his preanalytic, and his presocial state in order to learn more what man's "natural" state was. One would have to understand the tools of communication as they were in use then, not in the more articulate forms in which they are now the instruments of culture. Language, like life itself, metamorphosizes, and when it does, it covers much of the path over which it has moved. Language is far more than just a collection of symbols for holding in place the meanings of objects and relations. It is something which enriches itself as it accumulates. From general ideas, new conceptual forms shoot out like branches from a tree. But language accumulation is itself a reverse side of something even more important: a deepening and profoundly increasing human culture.

Tracing the rise of the use of symbol produces an invaluable insight into a study of man and his culture. But like the stone implements of Neolithic man, symbols reveal but a limited and partial side of the whole culture process. Even if one were able to discover all the antecedent conditions in man's primordial state which led to the use of symbol as the beginning of culture, there is yet the overwhelming fact of nature itself which must be understood in depth. Nature is not some mysterious cosmic force which created the phenomenological order while remaining detached from it. Nature is the phenomenological order itself, and man is a part of it. What one needs to know is not necessarily more of the manifold effects of this order already present in the world of appearances, but

---

[3] *Ibid.*, p. 27.

more of nature's inner coherence and underlying unity. Human culture incurs a humanization of the world, literally a clothing of the world with the effects of man's inner ingenuity and of his ideas of order. In this case, nature is involved in a double aspect of its fecundating activity. In one sense nature is the creator agent which produced mankind; in another sense it carries out a passive material role in creation in that it submits itself with all of its inner laws and precise regularities to man who, in a very literal sense, inherits the earth. The perennial question which philosophers ultimately ask is what man's real vocation on earth is.

Christian theology answers the question by saying that nature is the handiwork of God, the Creator, Who through His overflowing love created man to know and to love Him, and to participate in His glory. But the Christian position has been clouded for centuries because of a far too literal reading of the Genesis account of man's fall. That man became more open to temptation than he was in his primordial condition is quite an acceptable account of man's moral history, but this does not necessarily imply that he underwent moral disaster in one single event in the Garden of Eden. What is more likely a true reading of man's primordial condition is that his relation to God during this period was a deeply spiritual harmony and that man deliberately chose to estrange himself from God by concerning himself with matters of the world from which he could have remained spiritually free. That is, man chose to abandon his deep intuitive harmony in order to exercise his growing faculty of analytic reason. But while man's intellectual fascination with the natural world led him to a progressively deeper encounter with it, he discovered also that the world could be an alien and sometimes hostile force; and that this hostility would also be reflected in man's own personal behavior. Only through suffering and sorrow could he then begin to regain the spiritual freedom which he had lost.

The Creation story does not, in the Christian representation of it, indicate a total separation of God and the world. God does not abandon what He created because of man's disobedience. The central element of Christology is God's love of mankind. In the Incarnation, Christ takes on man's own physical nature and immerses Himself in its untold agony and suffering. The Incarnation of Christ in human flesh brought about a reawakening of man's spiritual nature, and it was through this that the spiritual redemption of the whole of mankind became possible. But salvation through Christ is not a rescuing of man's spiritual self from himself as a physical body. It is by no means a permanent release from the hold which biological passion makes upon man. Christ's Resurrection fulfills the meaning of the victory of spirit as life. It signifies that physical death no longer has final dominion over man. On the other hand, the victory of life over death is no mere gift which God gives to man. Because individual man holds within himself the principles of both life and death, he must face the problem of victory through his own choosing.

In a collective sense mankind was thus forced back upon itself to work out its own earthly problems. In the Middle Ages the instrument for working out these problems was the Medieval church, which saw the task of society largely as that of bringing about the will of God on earth. That the medieval community was one marked by an unusual internal harmony may have been the case, but the ruling clerics guarded its members carefully from what they regarded as a premature intellectualism. The revolt against this attitude which occurred in the Renaissance was noted for its revival of literature and art, and for the rise of science as a separate field not bound to the tradition of metaphysics. But the post-Renaissance period also incurred a growing tension among scholars which was to have its results in a revolutionary intellectualism not at all foreseen. Man's newly developed powers of reflection and analysis were beginning to make him increasingly confident in his power of conquest of his own natural environment. That this aroused serious misgivings and feelings of apprehension among the Scholastics was evident in the works of Giordano Bruno. Theology, the uncontested discipline which had ruled men's minds for so many centuries, stood now in danger of being discredited by science. That this feeling had but little foundation can be seen in the fact that Newton, Galileo, Bacon and others were no real threat to organized religious belief. But the fears of Bruno drove him nevertheless to the point of formulating a conception of God and creation which would remain unshaken in the face of any kind of argument based on scientific fact.

Bruno's answer to the challenge of science was his own brand of pantheism—a diremption of God in the world; God literally exposing his divine essence by becoming one with nature. For Bruno there was but one scale by which God's causal power descends in the production of things, and man's mind ascends in achieving a knowledge of them. But Bruno's position brought on a charge of unmitigated heresy. The world which men had learned to scorn was made to be in some way metaphysically equivalent to God's Divine Essence. Bruno's fate was to be burned at the stake for heresy.

As if it were some ironic aftermath, metaphysics began to lose its appeal. While science made no direct assault on either theology or philosophy, the fact that science could deal directly with empirical materials by way of a representative symbolism, and that it could systematically clarify its own methodology, opened the way to a mistrust of metaphysics as such. While a growing number of scholars were beginning to dispense with the idea of formal essences, ultimate causes and so forth, there was another element in Bruno's deductions which was subtle enough to escape much attention during his time, but which would reappear in nineteenth century idealism. This was the implication in his equivalence of God's creative power and man's knowing faculty that the activity of the Absolute as Pure Being could be brought in line with the causal structure of the world as created. The equivalence of God's way of creating and man's way of knowing could be brought about only through a mediating principle which is the causal world that, on the one hand, is created by God, and on the other hand, becomes known to man. The important point is that, if the logic with which the human mind receives and reconstructs the world of fact is equivalent to the causal activity under which the world of fact becomes real in human knowing, then logic and cause have a root identity. Moreover, there could be no real difference between the sufficient reason for a thing's existence, its *raison d'etre*, and its entire causal structure; for *cause* and *being* are, as far as their representative function is concerned, collapsed into a single idea. As a result the problem of knowledge then turns in a different direction. Once reasonable connections are understood and achieve coherence in man's ways of thinking it becomes possible to dispense with cause altogether.

After having been taken for granted for so many centuries, the idea of cause as something directly knowable in itself came under the withering attack of David Hume. Hume showed in a rather convincing manner that one can have no first hand or direct knowledge of cause. What are given as appearances are only successions of phenomena. While the causal connection is assumed to exist, one can never be sure that causation actually occurs. Since the goal of science is not to deal with abstract ideas but rather to formulate sets of laws or rules under which events can be predicted, the question of whether or not there is real cause cannot really affect the outcome of scientific investigation. However, one might now ask Hume if science does not also require the investigator to manipulate objects in a purposive manner. If that is the case then even his contesting the reality of cause becomes meaningless.

It was really mathematics rather than Hume's criticism which was mainly instrumental in man's releasing himself from such metaphysical concepts as *substance* and *cause*. In mathematics the idea of *function* can be held as a pure intelligible; it need have no direct reference or contact with bodies. Theoretical possibility could thus be explored quite apart from immediate practical results, and also far in advance of empirical confirmation. Whereas causal connections had been only supposed as existing in the concrete case, and their validity always vulnerable to the presence of contradictory evidence, functional relations present no such problem.

The effect of this substitution began to become apparent in Darwin's theory of evolution. It was here that the whole ontological position of man was thrown into a new light. In Greek philosophy and in its Christian synthesis by St. Thomas, man's distinctiveness in nature was the central focus. But the idea of an unbroken continuity in the natural order seriously undermined man's position of having a distinct essence peculiar to him alone. Not even the separation between mind and body could be regarded as secure against the inroads of evolutionary thinking. Nothing seemed to bar the way to which the idea of function could be applied. It could skirt any formal distinction between physical and mental phenomena since it was not rooted necessarily in either one.

In this reduction, however, the very essence of that which is sought for is again lost from sight. Function as such can be conceptualized without any reference to things which are actually functioning. When this kind of reduction is applied to social data the process itself turns out to be a self-defeating one. The social theory which is presumed to follow such an application turns out to be meaningless because the main object of the investigation has become obscure. Social theory is founded on the idea of intersubjectivity; on the modes of communication and other forms of interpersonal exchange which people carry on. But when it is carried out by way of an analysis of functions, then subjectivity *per se* disappears completely. Any wish that this new means of elaborating the data of inquiry might furnish an entirely new set of clues for understanding human nature turns out to be a false hope. It is possible to suggest, as Gustav Fechner does, that there is a psychic element in plants which extends itself upwards into animal behavior, which is, in turn, reducible to various kinds of tropism-heliotropism, geotropism and phototropism. But this means of resolving data falls short when there is a call for self-specification. The function device serves very well as long as no qualitative differences in data have to be taken into account. Functional connections can be rationalized in numerous sets of related variables. The same set of data might be held as invariant under a number of transformations of the means for identifying and quantifying them. In empirical inquiry it is quite possible to hold to the idea of a fundamental unity in nature, especially when the nature of what is sought for persists as primarily physical in all its attributes. But, as Cassirer points out,

> The distinguishing trait we are looking for is not a physical but a *functional* distinction. . . . For the decisive change lies, not in the emergence of new features and properties, but in the characteristic *change of function* which all determinations undergo as soon as we pass from the animal world to the human world. . . . The "freedom" which man is able to wrest for himself does not imply that he has removed himself from nature, from her being and operations. He cannot overturn or break through the organic limits which are fixed for him just as for the other living beings. But within these limits, indeed by means of

them, he fashions a breadth and self-sufficiency of movement which is accessible and attainable only by him.[4]

The deep cleft between the two areas of performance denotes the wide difference between the strictly physiological and
the cultural aspects of mankind. To be sure, mental processes
are shaped and guided by what is given in appearances, but the
power to organize data is not. Cultural conditions do refer to
the physical world, but as instruments on which its melody is
played. Cultural phenomena are a set of experiences which did
not exist before man appeared on the scene, and it is by these
means that he has come to acknowledge his privileged position in the world. These experiences could not occur except
through the activities of consciousness and of man's reflective
and vocal apparatus; activities which denote the very *being*
of subjectivity and, as such, are out of reach of any mechanical
or mathematical formulation.

They are out of reach because culture concepts originate
in what is highly personal and subjective; not in what is given
in appearances. Also, inasmuch as cultural expressions occur
only through the media of the culture itself—through the symbolism appropriate for each area, the instrumental world is
called on to convey these symbols in some manner hopefully
adequate to the task. Culture develops and occurs only through
reciprocal personal transaction. One can speak and reason only
with some other person—not with that which might have consciousness and a vocal apparatus but lacks the power of rational expression. From the one strata of the life process to
the other, from the physiological to the cultural, the whole
nature of species relations undergoes a profound change. There
are, Cassirer points out, some human reactions to nonhuman
stimuli that evoke perceptual experiences in which the human
response is an emotive or a habitual reaction. But culture

---
[4] *Ibid.*, p. 73.

31

forms, in spite of their immense diversity, are active expression forms. "They are not simply events," he says, "which play themselves out within and upon our bodies, but are, as it were, specific energies. It is through the exercise of these energies that the world of culture takes form—the form of language, art and religion." [5]

It would be an obvious advantage to the investigator if culture concepts could be reduced to a single kind of symbolic representation. But if the field were so narrowed one would have to be content with results which would be equally narrow. Any investigation of culture which consistently reduced all culture symbols to the fewest possible types would be self-defeating. The riddle which one tries to solve in cultural inquiry is not one which is concerned with discovering some occult mysteries, some intellectual phantoms indigenous to culture itself. The object of inquiry is man himself, and the diversity of culture symbols is a clue to the whole depth of personality which the philosopher can hardly overlook.

The fact that man is organically continuous with the biological world is certainly evident in that his basic cellular composition and his circulatory and nervous systems have correlates with other forms of animal life. But it is not enough simply to regard man as another link in the chain of being. When man is included biologically with the rest of living species it is with the understanding that his own biological processes occur similarly elsewhere. But human existence can be understood in terms of its uniqueness only by acknowledging that it is itself, within the entire biological energy field, an enormous setting. Whereas lower animal life has developed in accordance with the presence or absence of optimum conditions for survival, human life has spread itself over most of the earth. The reason for the much larger possibilities for

---

[5] *Ibid.*, p. 110.

32

survival in man's case does not lie in a far greater range of instinctive adaptation. But it does lie in the power of his reflective apparatus, and in his power to cause the results of his reflection to congeal into ways of extending his control over what is sometimes a hostile environment.

Looking for the true essence of man in routine instances of behavior tends to be rather fruitless because, for the most part, these yield only fragmented details having no fundamental coherence. What one looks for in a study of culture symbols are traces of an ontological perspective which might also indicate something of the ontological setting which converged within itself to produce man in all his varied expression forms. For while culture concepts may be thought of as sealed off from symbols having no cultural reference, these concepts have not arisen out of nothing. These are active expression forms which arose at a very late hour in the world's evolutionary story. The actual budding of human consciousness took many centuries to be achieved; but the fact that it was achieved leads one to believe that the creative forces which brought it forth did not totally disappear but are somehow present and somehow surface in the ingenuity of human artistic performance and works of genius. Human behavior leaves its mark and its energy impress wherever it moves. Every detail of art, every literary form, every nuance in musical composition, and also, the handling of practical affairs, are the work of a deep-rooted logic of consciousness which is canalized in man as mind.

If the mystery of existence remains obscure, it is not because it is necessarily unknowable, but rather because man has not yet discovered the terms by which it can be brought into clear focus. Modern research continues to make a steady increase in the fund of knowledge of man's physical self. But the human psyche has always been far too elusive to be completely analyzed by the rather coarse methods of either intro-

33

spective or behaviorist psychology. The reason for this is quite clear. The psyche cannot be located in any precise region of the body, and it is not, therefore, something which can be surgically removed. It is something which has to be handled by dealing with the whole person. Furthermore, this is something which applies in a very special way to the human figure: the more completely a unit of essence encapsulates existential fact, the more unknowable it becomes by customary procedures of inquiry. To know something well one must be able to make a clear distinction between the content which is to be known and the method by which it is known. In the human case, content and methods are both encapsulated within the same figure, and the separation is, therefore, impossible.

Another difficulty involved in a study of man is the circular nature of the situation. Everything in psyche behavior must be situated in a field if it is to be understood. Yet it is psyche behavior which makes this field to be what it is. By following a purely ontic description, it is impossible to relate one to the other to give any meaning because the answers sought for have a greater ontological depth than surface symbols can reach. One can, for example, reduce all moral dispositions, as did Dewey, to "habits," and one can reduce all heuristic passions to psychological drives tending toward some kind of satisfaction. But such reductions place man squarely back in the animal world, a position which is quite incompatible with the fact that man is conducting the investigation. Such reductions do not by any means obviate the fact that man is a species which continually presses forward to seek and to hold all that is within its reach. It is called "research" when inquiry is carried out in a highly elaborate fashion. But research is carried out in some way by practically everyone. It is this which goes on when one is trying to secure a more complete existential bond between himself and what is about him. Much of it is private and personal; on the other hand, much of it is ordinary and readily shared. But in either case it is a matter of the external submitting to the internal, to the logic and the design of mind, and even to the urge of passion.

Every type of philosophy is an attempt to assess or to reassess the existential situation. Every novel approach has managed to gain the attention of some men of philosophy and also some of science. The purpose here is not to produce a compendium of philosophical positions, but to examine what these have brought to bear on the question of existence. No one of these can be regarded as a complete ontological synthesis of man in the natural, and perhaps also, in the supernatural orders. In fact there is in some cases a rejection of ontology altogether. However, whether philosophers recognize or admit an ontology or not, there is always at least some attempt at self-certification of the method. Whether or not a philosophy manages to envelop very much of the whole existential situation, in order for a structured system of thought to be a philosophy at all, there must be some attempt to make its position secure.

CHAPTER II

The Naturalist Answer

PHILOSOPHICAL NATURALISM originated from a number of sources. Coming rather late in the historical development of philosophy, it can count among its antecedents many of the specialized lines of inquiry which sprang from the main trunk of philosophy itself. Although not contributing directly to the naturalist movement, mechanistic physics, under the far reaching influence of Sir Isaac Newton, did lay the groundwork for the reception several centuries later of philosophical naturalism. The growth of physics was due in a large sense to the disclosure of certain mechanical regularities in the interaction of natural bodies. But physicists were able to make remarkable progress in their field mainly because they could confine their efforts to such matters which could be empirically verified. That this progress would inspire a growing confidence in the scientific method is what one would expect. On the other hand there were certain philosophers in the twentieth century who assumed that their own discipline could and should proceed in the same manner. There were also certain physicists, such as Heisenberg, who were beginning to question the universal validity of mechanistic causes as irreducible forms of explanation. But by this time naturalist philosophy, growing bit by bit, had begun to bypass the idea of mechanistic causes. Since the time of Hume's critical examination of whether one can actually know causal phenomena directly, it had been considered much safer to avoid the dogmatic issue and to concentrate instead on what was empirically at hand. Also, naturalist philosophy came ultimately to deal with the content of science only in an indirect way. That is, it has presented its case, not so much on the content of science, as on its method.

There is a tendency among philosophers to fix the great ages of philosophy as occurring before and after the period of Descartes. But it would be pointless to try to trace the origin of all contemporary philosophy to his work. One development which did give naturalism a chance to grow was an increasing distrust in metaphysical and theological explanations. With his subjectivist postulate Descartes had contributed much to the weakening of metaphysics—something which he neither wished nor intended to do. Realizing that his subjectivist position— that one can never be certain that body and mind interact in any way—seriously endangered the certainty of any metaphysical position, Descartes tried to rectify matters through a strong theological position. If a just and veracious God exists, Descartes contended, He would not deceive man by creating a world of mind and a world of material bodies which were not oriented to one another. Accordingly, Descartes then set out to prove to his own satisfaction that God exists.

Later philosophers, however, were not entirely concerned either with the God problem or with the mind-body one. In the nineteenth century Auguste Comte was prepared to eliminate both metaphysics and theology, and to replace both with what he believed to be a positive science which would apply equally to social and to physical matters. For Comte, the growing conquest of the physical world was a preliminary step to the application of the method of science to the whole gamut of natural affairs. He constructed a hierarchy of the separate scientific disciplines, with mathematics as the foundation subject, and with astronomy, physics, chemistry and biology following in that order. For Comte, each applied science was a certain kind of physics. Astronomy was celestial physics; physics proper and chemistry were the terrestrial forms of this basic subject; biology was organic physics, and the crowning discipline was social physics, or sociology. This would supply the fresh insights for a new emerging era of social positivism. But Comte's writings lacked the subtlety which often makes a new social dogma intellectually attractive. His priesthood of sociological experts too closely resembled actual reformers who had been heard for some time. Then also, his own country France, as well as England and America, was far too engrossed in the pursuit of newly won liberties to accept readily the blind social cooperation which Comte's system demanded. His social positivism did not receive much public interest or acclaim in his own time. But it survived amazingly well by infiltration, by reappearing in various disguises in later theoretical formulations.

New strains in philosophy tend often to appear as do manifestations of charisma; that is, they appear when the truths of older systems seem to be in doubt. One rather significant influence on the growth of naturalism was a negative one—a rejection of any concept of an immaterial, immortal soul whose nurture was man's primary concern. Naturalism derived its positive content from stressing the goodness of the experience of natural man. Its avowed purpose, as expressed by a number of naturalist philosophers, was the elevation of earthly life toward realizing its fullest potential for happiness. In the meantime, a growing secularization of society had been creating a metaphysical void which needed filling. The void in this case was the lack of clearly defined secularist goals. Popular opinion had been generally in support of the position that secularist goals existed and were also discoverable. Because of the aura regarding the uplifting effects of education, it was quite logical to suppose that public education should be the instrument through which such goals could be discovered and carried out.

During the latter part of the nineteenth century public education was a growing novel institution, an instrument of support for self-government in a new and expanding social frontier. Jefferson had made it clear that a democratic society did not exist *per accidens,* that it would not be called into being just by a perfunctory choice on the part of those who could live under it. There was a price attached to self-government—an enlightened electorate. The task of public education, of enlightening or illuminating the minds of those who were now set upon the path of self-rule, was accordingly clear. The meaning of the term "enlightened," however, does not carry with it a universal assent. It might mean the achievement of peace, harmony and security for all. But it could also mean a heightened view of one's own self-interest. Unfortunately it was this latter view which was frequently given as the main purpose of education in the early part of the twentieth century. Quite in line with the thinking of the President who remarked that "the business of America is business," there were many exhortations given to high school and college students about the commercial value of education. Advanced learning was an almost assured way of becoming rich. This was the beautiful dream which was so pervasive in the thinking of the "twenties." But a very severe depression shattered the hopes and expectations of those who had been caught up in this great promise, and shattered also the dream.

It is not that public education is ineffectual, or that it was ineffectual then. But the holocaust of misery which descended on American society during the first period of the thirties made it quite clear that something had been seriously wrong with the prevailing point of view. American civilization during the nineteenth century had cut itself loose from much of the heritage of European tradition. It had been a melting pot, but

39

one in which many of the old cultures were being melted down without a corresponding refinement of a new one. It is true that many of the old traditions and forms of culture were preserved and kept somewhat intact, but these were retained mainly by ethnic communities in which there was a strong interest for keeping traditional forms of culture alive. The reasons for the mass migrations in the nineteenth century were private and personal, and in some cases also negative. In some instances migration was prompted by a wish to escape from the hard lines of social stratification which had been characteristic of life in the homeland. Life in America was a fresh promise of opportunity, and also something of a release from the growing tide of nationalism in central Europe. If there was no great movement toward a national cousciousness in America in the nineteenth century and in the early part of the twentieth, it could well have been because suggestions of intense national interest were looked upon with suspicion and even hostility. However, the pursuit of individual liberty unguided by any humanist social ideal did not guarantee the peace, harmony and prosperity which some thought would necessarily follow. The idea that "the business of America is business" echoed much contemporary thought, but it turned out to be quite a false idea. Nineteenth century liberalism had promoted the growth of *laissez faire* economics, but an increasing disparity between the fortunes of the rich and the poor was causing the liberal in the twentieth century to suspect *laissez faire* capitalism of having certain inherited incompatible tendencies. The apparent indifference of many people in industry and in politics toward natural values was causing others to voice the feeling that American society, although a young, fresh civilization, was already sick and beyond saving and that mercy called for its quick extermination. Very clearly any new prophet who had anything to say about social matters, particularly education, would soon be heard.

JOHN DEWEY'S *RECONSTRUCTION IN PHILOSOPHY*

The naturalist philosophy of John Dewey began in the metaphysical void induced in the twentieth century by the growing schism between idealist philosophy and practical concerns. His social philosophy comes to a real focus in the *Reconstruction in Philosophy*. In the "Introduction" he supplies several premises for his arguments in the main body of the text. These are, first, recent scientific and technological advances have greatly altered the human situation socially; second, the moral directives which have come down from the older philosophies and ecclesiastical institutions were not adequate for giving positive intellectual direction to people living in a scientific rather than in a prescientific age; and, third, there is an urgent need for reconstructive work in philosophy which would bring it to the level of a discipline capable of dealing effectively with the practical needs of man. In his own words, Dewey says that philosophy "Must undertake to do for the development of inquiry into human affairs and hence into morals what the philosophers of the last few centuries did for the promotion of scientific inquiry into physical and physiological conditions and aspects of human life." [1] For the direction which this "reconstruction" in philosophy is to take, he said that it

> can be nothing less than the work of developing, of forming, of producing (in the literal sense of that word) the intellectual instrumentalities which will progressively direct moral inquiry into the deeply and exclusively human—that is to say, moral—facts of the present scene and situation. [2]

---

[1] John Dewey, *Reconstruction in Philosophy*. Enlarged edition (Boston: The Beacon Press, 1948), p. xxii.
[2] *Ibid.*, p. xxvii.

41

Here is a twentieth century echo of the optimistic expectation with which Francis Bacon plunged into the task of producing the *Novum Organum*. Bacon hoped to restore a philosophy grown stagnant through years of contentious quibbling over idle matters with one having the vitality of an inductive discipline. Dewey, however, intended to go much further than just reconstructing philosophy along the lines of scientific inquiry. He intended to utilize both the method and the findings of science to reassess the human situation and to relocate its goals. Whereas Bacon was concerned with finding an inductive means for more thoroughly comprehending nature, Dewey invested the method which he tried to develop with significant moral possibilities. In contrast with the positions held by the older religions which, in his estimate, regarded man as inherently corrupt, he took the opposing view that science had given man both the wisdom and the means for indefinite moral progress. Rather than viewing man as so inherently depraved that he can look only toward a suprahuman, supernatural authority, Dewey aimed philosophy in another direction: "that of systematic endeavor to see and to state the constructive significance for the future of man wrought primarily by the new science." [3] For Dewey, an Absolute Reality stood literally outside of time and outside of natural experience. He insisted that once philosophy surrendered its concern with this idea it would find compensation in "enlightening the moral forces which move mankind and in contributing to the aspirations of men to a more ordered and intelligent happiness." [4] Accordingly, for Dewey the very first task in this direction was recasting the idea of nature so that it could be subdued to human purposes rather than being forever made to fit the designs of metaphysics and theology.

Dewey began his task of reconstruction by citing the de-

[3] *Ibid.*, p. xxxiv.
[4] *Ibid.*, p. 26.

velopment of psychology out of biological concepts which "makes possible a new scientific formulation of the nature of experience."[5] He makes this formulation from the close alliance between perceptive operations and the modifications in the environment of the organisms which follow these operations. "The living creature," he wrote, "undergoes, suffers the consequences of its own behavior. The close connection between doing and suffering or undergoing forms what we call experience."[6]

A second step which he makes is closing the gap between knowledge and sensation. Knowledge is conceived as an interaction of the organism and its environment. Whatever there is of it is involved in the process through which life evolves and is sustained. Sense activity is a stimulus of action whether reflective or reflexive. The whole process comes now to be acknowledged as the phenomenon of experience. "We use our past experiences to construct new and better ones in the future. The very fact of experience thus includes the process by which it directs itself in its own betterment."[7]

Here Dewey lays bare his debt to Hegel. It would be grossly unfair to blame Hegel for the deliberate twist which Dewey made in the preceding pair of statements, but the reification of "experience" as some temporal absolute is an unmistakable Hegelian influence. Any question which one might have concerning how far naturalist philosophy could go while paying attention only to the method and content of science seems to be answered here. When Dewey says "We use our past experiences . . ." he affirms the duality between what man is and what he does. But in the very next sentence this duality is conveniently ignored. It is now something called "experience" which is directing itself to its own betterment rather than *man*

[5] *Ibid.*, p. 84.
[6] *Ibid.*, p. 86.
[7] *Ibid.*, p. 95.

or *person* as the term "we" implied in the first sentence. But how could "experience" be a subject or the "fact of experience" direct itself to its own betterment?

In reifying "experience" as something autonomous, as an ultimate social referent, Dewey's thinking is a case of reverse Hegelianism. For Hegel, the world process was the work of an inexorable Logic of the Absolute, self-externalized and emptied into time. It was the Logic of God's *Becoming;* of God externalizing Himself by expressing the truth of his essence in Creation, and in this way becoming fully conscious of Himself as God. The figure given as representing the effective presence of God in the world was Spirit. Although the truth of Spirit is recognized in terms of its objective determination —in terms of what is given as concretely real to human consciousness, human consciousness is itself a mode through which Spirit deploys itself as Universal Consciousness. That is, it is through man's freedom as subjectivity that Spirit is creative of new forms of objective determination.[8] But Dewey assigns this creativity to something other than man—in this case something called "experience," and perhaps because "experience" does not carry with it all of the troublesome problems about man's nature.

It is man's freedom which was such a perplexing problem for Dewey. Man's freedom was clearly the root condition responsible for the many social ills which he hoped to resolve

---

[8] The figure which Hegel used to express this divided aspect of Spirit is the Notion. The Notion is Spirit as Consciousness in both its alternate moments of objective and subjective truth; as Spirit *an-sich-selbst* (in-itself) in the former case and *fur-sich-selbst* (for-itself) in the latter. As objective truth Spirit has revealed itself externally in the world of physical fact and in human ways of knowing. But human ways of knowing are, for Hegel, also God's ways of knowing Himself since man is God's own creation. In his human physiology man bears the mark of objective truth; but man is also the means for an infinite subjectivity in that qua consciousness he bears an essential mark of Spirit—that of freedom.

44

by means of his proposed "inquiry." But social inquiry could not be easily rationalized if it is assumed to originate by way of the same freedom in man which makes man morally vulnerable. Presenting man as both the culprit and the savior in society involved an insurmountable problem which could only result in polarizing man and society in the one role or the other. Dewey could not resort to a metaphysical reconciliation of man and society because he had already denied metaphysics; and he could not rely on any concept of salvation by Grace since he had already denied theology. Accordingly that which involved both man and society—social "experience"—was to be the instrument of social direction. Even though it involved man's sinful condition, experience is sinless in itself. Hence social direction is something which is to be wrought out of experience, and experience is Dewey's own absolute. It is the all-embracing whole within which man's moral destiny is somehow conceived. "Although," Dewey says,

. . . this self-creating and self-regulating experience is still largely technological, rather than truly artistic or human, yet what has been achieved contains the guaranty of the possibility of an intellectual administering of experience. The limits are moral and intellectual due to the defects in our good will and knowledge.[9]

Dewey's abhorrence of any bipolarity of the real and ideal worlds comes to the fore in this collapsing of distinctions between subject and object, or between experience as such and that which undergoes experience. So intent does he seem to be to eliminate from practical philosophy all vestiges of ideality that traces of formality are likewise suspect. Logic cannot be dispensed with, for it is an undisputed guide to thought. But he imposes his rule upon this too. "If thought or intelligence,"

---

[9] *Ibid.,* p. 95.

he wrote, "is the means of intentional reconstruction of experience, then logic as an account of the procedure of thought is not purely formal. It is not confined to laws of formally correct reasoning apart from the truth of subject matter." [10] Here again is an echo from Hegel. In saying that thought or intelligence is the means of intentional reconstruction of experience Dewey is stating something of which people are generally aware; intelligence is a kind of tool which a human ego uses in exploring possible forms of experience. There is no attempt so far to invest intelligence itself with any ego power. But when he adds the statement that logic is not purely formal, that it is not confined to laws of formally correct reasoning apart from the truth of subject matter, he is in a negative fashion implying that logic has some inner integrity of its own. The implication is far too strong to be ignored that, for Dewey, logic is not just the law of thought—a guide to truth—but that it produces truth in and through itself. In Dewey's own words the function of thought is said to increase from "intentional reconstruction" to a "deliberate reorganization" of experience. *Person, thought, logic* and the *self* are all swept up into the general idea of a self-determining process, a clear analogue to Hegel's Notion, which is presumed to be able to advance by its own power toward self-clarification once the correct methodology is established. But what is it which certifies the correctness of methodology? Is his logic self-certifying? This is apparently not the case, for at one point he says that "light is thrown by the origin of thinking upon a logic which shall be a method of intelligent guidance of experience." [11] As a method alone, it is obviously incapable of separating what is intelligent from what is not. He develops the idea of "thought as construction" as an instrumentalist theory which "only attempts to state with some scrupulousness *where* the value is

---

10 *Ibid.*, p. 134.
11 *Ibid.*, p. 138.

found and to prevent its being sought for in the wrong place."[12] But again, what is it which does the *finding* of value, and what is it which prevents value from being sought for in the wrong place?

There is some evidence that Dewey is now beginning to waver from his earlier position on the supremacy of method. He proposes now that investigation in social affairs should be confined to those people who "are in unobstructed co-operation with other social occupations, sensitive to other's problems and transmitting results to them for wider application in action." [13] Here he seems to be falling back in search of some more secure ground than reconstructed experience. There is a genuine appeal, not to method, but to people who use method. "The only guarantee," he writes, "of impartial disinterested inquiry is the social sensitiveness of the inquirer to the needs and problems of those with whom he is associated." [14]

One need not gloss over what is an incompatibility, and a logical incompatibility at that, of "social sensitiveness" and "disinterested inquiry" in the same observer. The main concern is that of discovering how far Dewey is able to push the idea of an autonomous logic expressing itself through experience. He tends always to hold "experience" as the central focus, even in reference to abstraction. "Abstraction," he says, "is liberation." [15] But what is it which is liberated? There is some hint about what he means when he states that "Abstraction sets free some factor so that it may be used. Generalization is the use." [16] But again, what is the "factor" of which he is speaking? Is it something belonging to the class of "eternal species or occult essences" which he discredits in another

---

[12] *Ibid.*, p. 148.
[13] *Ibid.*, p. 147.
[14] *Ibid.*, p. 147.
[15] *Ibid.*, p. 150.
[16] *Ibid.*, p. 151.

paragraph? One can, of course, conclude that the "factor" is an element of thought, something which is handled in the logical use of data. But that does end the question whether logic qua experience or conversely, experience qua logic is some autonomous, spiritualized whole which is entirely self-originating in its activity.

Two aspects of Dewey's conception of truth are indeed pertinent at this point. The first is his casting it entirely in an adverbial sense as a mode of acting. "Its active, dynamic function is the all-important thing about it, and in the quality of activity induced by it lies all of its truth and falsity."[17] By this description he apparently hoped to safeguard the concept of the true from any association with "fixed" structures. Verification lies in consequences; no other criterion of truth is admissible. With this one might agree, but only with the stipulation that there are some means available for determining the *quality* of an activity or the value content of a consequence. The second concerns his method of solidifying the ground of the first. Perhaps he was aware that "confirmation in works and consequences" might involve works and consequences which are in themselves suspect. These lead toward something which he calls "our end." They are legitimate only if "our end" is likewise so. But to make the "end" above repute he must find something which arouses a negative social response so that his concept of a legitimate end acquires, by contrast, a positive shading. His target is the satisfaction of a private comfort, a meeting of purely personal needs. "But the satisfaction in question," he says, "means the satisfaction of the needs and conditions of the problem out of which the idea, the purpose and method of action arises. It includes public and objective conditions."[18]

What are *public* and *objective* conditions, and what does

17 *Ibid.*, p. 156.
18 *Ibid.*, p. 157.

one mean by the "satisfaction of the needs and conditions of the problem"? The original purpose of Dewey's new logic was leading individual man toward a more ordered and intelligent happiness. But individual man now seems to have disappeared from the main focus of his thinking. Man has been replaced by something given as the "problem." A "problem," however, has no bones or flesh, no reason or consciousness. Dewey seems to have fallen into that intellectual trap which is such a hazard for social theorists who begin with a denial of metaphysics; individual man and society cannot be reconciled in any ethical synthesis. Society cannot be rationalized except at man's expense; it is affirmed as something "public" or as "objective," and these terms supposedly convey what is good and true as opposed to what is base in personal pursuit. Man, on the other hand, expresses his integral selfhood, his individuality, only by standing apart from the whole; by traits of "nonconformance," or by opposing himself to the "establishment." A new logic, intended to be a means for the realization of a more complete human goodness, has now come to point at something which is not human at all. Except for those cases in which there are "men and women of good will," individual man as such is incapable of making progress toward a high level of ethical integrity. Only by being transformed in depth so that he conforms to the needs and conditions of the "problem" does man become truly moral. Something designated as "public" comes to be the supreme reference for moral matters. It comes to be the supreme guide for intelligent thinking and action.

MORAL RECONSTRUCTION

In the early part of the *Reconstruction in Philosophy* the method used was intended to emulate that of science. One can hardly censure Dewey for this. It is axiomatic, in realist philosophy especially, that the facts must be taken into account. If taking these into account calls for a refinement in method by a more direct encounter with factual data, one has little choice other than to concur. One can, however, question whether such a revision in method alone can bring the ken of philosophy within reach of social issues which are apropos to and contemporaneous with the scientific, even the technological, temper of the age.

Everywhere throughout the *Reconstruction* there are unmistakable signs of Dewey's deep moral concern for man in the social situation. But in what one has seen of his philosophy so far he flatly evades any reason, any real purpose, for man's acting in a moral way. He insists that the key to moral recovery in the social situation lies in intelligent thinking and acting, while at the same time denying that man's intellect has any natural object. For him, moral truth is always situational. But what establishes the verity of the situation? Self-interest is, for him, a fact of existence having no ontological referent—no ground for governing the intension of this sort of concern. But it is a fact all too obvious for him to try to avoid. "When the play of interest is eliminated," he asks, "what remains? What concrete moving forces can be found?" Later in the same paragraph he says, "Interests are specific and dynamic; they are the natural terms of any concrete social thinking. But they are damned beyond recovery when they are identified with the things of a petty selfishness." [19]

Again, Dewey ought to be commended for his moral sensitivity—for his genuine concern regarding the totum of being which is mankind. Yet while he proposes concern regarding man in the social situation, he refrains from citing any specific moral situations, difficulties, or evils so that the reader is left wondering what he could be referring to. He complains that

---

[19] *Ibid.*, p. 195.

the belief in fixed values bred a division of ends into one set which are intrinsic in themselves and into another in which ends are instrumental. He prefers the instrumental ones because these lead to intrinsic goods in the concrete case. Then he exhibits a distrust of concrete goods considered intrinsic in themselves and of private ends which are regarded as instrumental.

One tangible aspect of life which appears to give content to Dewey's ethical theory is that of "growth." Growth toward what? Here again, he will not say. He speaks of the "ever-enduring process of perfecting, maturing, refining [which] is the aim in living."[20] But why speak of perfecting if *perfection* has no meaning? Why use the term "maturation" if the term "mature" has no practical significance? Like so many other philosophers who grapple with this problem, Dewey turns also in the direction of the mechanics of social organization and control. But this is not in line with Plato's method of trying to see in the State the image of man. A philosopher who refuses to say what man *is* can hardly be expected to say anything about man's image. Dewey supposed three general social theories: (1) the State existing to serve the individual, (2) the individual existing to realize the purpose of the State, and (3) the organic theory wherein both State and individual are each substantial entities requiring the support of each other. He sees the latter theory as answering most of the objections raised against the other two. However, even this one does not satisfy him entirely—there is no provision for "growth." As a mere *status quo* expression, it is lacking in empirical vitality.

Dewey seems to be somewhat at a loss about how to reconcile the brute facts of human behavior with his own optimistic expectations regarding the scientific method as a tool of moral inquiry. His momentary concern with statecraft does

---

[20] *Ibid.*, p. 177.

not provide him with a way out of this impasse. But following this brief encounter with the political side of existence he turns once again to reencounter man, at least in an individual, if not in a personal, sense. "Individuality," he says, "in a social and moral sense is something to be wrought out. It means initiative, inventiveness, varied resourcefulness, assumption of responsibility in choice of belief and conduct. These are not gifts but achievements." [21] His statement—"The interest in individual moral improvement and the social interest in objective reform of economic and political conditions are identified" [22]—ought also to be considered. One wonders if Dewey is now moving toward the position that there is inherent within man's own nature an ordering principle for the society in which he lives, moves and completes his being. This is the metaphysical position which he has been apparently trying to avoid, but there are occasional hints here and there that this may be the case. He acknowledges, for one thing, the limit of the significance of organization. He says that "It is a means of promoting association, of multiplying effective points of contact between persons, directing their intercourse into the modes of greatest fruitfulness." [23] Does this mean, perhaps, that he is now moving toward the natural law position of Aristotle and St. Thomas? Hardly so. In a later paragraph he states that "Only in association with fellows does he [man] become a conscious center of experience." [24] What appears here is that it is "experience" which is the main focus rather than man. It is philosophically safe for Dewey to use that term; in using it one does not have to deal with the problem of moral evaluation—a problem which must always be faced in the case of man.

---

[21] *Ibid.*, p. 194.
[22] *Ibid.*, p. 196.
[23] *Ibid.*, p. 206.
[24] *Ibid.*, p. 207.

Now and then, glinting through his attempts at philosophical reconstruction there is the practical Dewey, talking in plain, ordinary language about matter-of-fact details of existence. "Conditions and events are neither to be fled from nor passively acquiesced in; they are to be utilized and directed." [25] Here is a wholesome perspective toward contemporary life with which one could hardly disagree. "Since changes," he wrote, "are going on anyway, the great thing is to learn enough about them so that we be able to lay hold of them and turn them in the direction of our desires." [26] Enough of Dewey's honest intentions have been seen for one to assume that he did not mean unrationalized or wanton desires but rather man's genuine moral and social reform. However, instead of showing what the new logic would be and how it would work, he seems to be describing the conduct of people who are already acting intelligently.

There is one assumption in this work which one would not be prone to contradict: that man is able to act more intelligently than he has in the past. The function of an improved logic is that of clarifying the issues involved, and this seems to be the principal feature of naturalist philosophy. But after the issues have been clarified, one is still faced with the dictates of his own intelligence. Dewey apparently realizes the ineffectualness of logic alone in coping with this problem. It is perhaps for this reason that he has to augment the new discipline with the added factor of people who have the proper moral disposition for putting his reconstructed social philosophy into effect.

What can be salvaged in Dewey's philosophy, what throws light on the continuing problem of social reconstruction, is his stressing of experimental intelligence. The work of intellect is analytical, but it is also synthetic in its operations. That is,

---

[25] *Ibid.*, p. 116.
[26] *Ibid.*, p. 116.

it does not merely resolve issues into their simplest, their most elementary components; it also recomposes them into such constructs that people make judgments; but it is the *person,* not the logic, which makes the judgment. Dewey was certainly aware that logic is not some disembodied force, but he nevertheless seems always to have wavered between absolutizing intelligence on one hand, and on the other, of resolving the whole phenomenon of people acting intelligently under the general idea of "experience" progressively working toward its own betterment.

A second fact concerning naturalist philosophy is the attention which it has focused on concrete conditions of existence. It is no doubt true that Dewey's rejection of metaphysics and theology could only have been accomplished by ignoring the more pertinent facts of existence, especially of human existence. The work of consciousness, of analytic reason, of man's love for his fellows, of the good will in which Dewey himself had so much faith are all facts of behavior which are not explainable by scientific terminology alone. He did, however, expose some of the prolonged failings of many who profess to be religious. One of these is their prolonged indifference to grievous matters in the concrete case; as if one ought to look at world tragedy as a punishment from God with which individual man need not greatly concern himself; as if the law of personal salvation in eternity does not bear in any way on the law of society in time.

NAGEL'S *LOGIC WITHOUT METAPHYSICS*

The way which philosophical naturalism leaves open to itself is the natural world, bereft of any necessary connection with theology or metaphysics. It is the natural world as it is given in appearances. The one tool with which naturalist philosophers presume to carry out their intellectual encounter

lence of knowing and being—that is, becoming. In the case of Creation, and especially Creation *ex nihilo,* the problems of knowing and of becoming are insoluble by ordinary analysis. Creation *ex nihilo* means literally to become out of nothing, to be brought into existence out of no previously existing reality; and hence there is in such a case no causal series which can be supposed. Hegel's Logic of the Absolute is the one philosophical system intended as an exposition of the Absolute in its moments of self-reflecting creativity; moments in which there is an utter identicalness between thinking and being.

Compared with Hegel, the Vienna school of logical positivists constituted an opposite polarization in logical theory. It is true that the group of men who identified themselves as logical positivists were interested in pursuing logic as an independent discipline, coming under no one system of metaphysics or of science; and in this sense they were following somewhat the same course as Hegel. But logic for them was in no sense dialectical, and their apparent unconcern for the world of physical fact, as if the single purpose of philosophy was logical analysis and nothing else, caused the application of logic to be restricted to a very narrow area of speculation. In this regard the philosophical world is now indebted to contemporary naturalism for forcing the problem of the meaning of human existence out into the open and for reestablishing its relevance in nontheistic philosophy.

The position of contemporary naturalism in the post-Dewey period is, nonetheless, somewhat unclear. According to Ernest Nagel, naturalism does not specify any set of substantive principles for explaining a set of concrete happenings in terms other than those used in the natural sciences. It does not "offer its general view of nature and man as the product of some special philosophical mode of knowing." [28] Its own ac-

---

[28] Ernest Nagel, *Logic Without Metaphysics* (Glencoe, Illinois: The Free Press, 1956), p. 6.

count of things is a distillation of the knowledge acquired in the other sciences.

Naturalism does, however, have a set of fundamental assertions from which its position is developed. "The first," Nagel says, "is the existential causal primacy of organized matter in the executive order of nature." [29] All phenomena have their origin in the behavior of spatio-temporal bodies operating within themselves and upon other bodies by way of their internal structures and their external relations. The second thesis is really an affirmation of the first, which is that:

> the manifest plurality and variety of things, of their qualities and their functions, are an irreducible feature of the cosmos, not a deceptive appearance cloaking some more homogeneous "ultimate reality" or trans-empirical substance, and that the sequential orders in which events occur or the manifold relations of dependence in which things exist are *contingent* connections, not the embodiment of a fixed and unified pattern of logically necessary links.[30]

Where does the naturalism of Nagel lead from here? That there are gradations of existence, that there are diverse modes of action, relations of men, aspirations, he readily admits. He also speaks of "integrated systems of bodies, such as biological organisms, which have the capacity to maintain themselves and the direction of their characteristic activities." [31] It is only present experience which counts. There is no room for the concept of a teleological order of nature.[32]

---

[29] *Ibid.*, p. 7.
[30] *Ibid.*, p. 7.
[31] *Ibid.*, p. 8.
[32] Nagel states: "But there is no positive evidence, and much negative evidence, for the supposition that all existential structures are teleological systems in this sense, or for the view that whatever oc-

So far, Nagel's naturalist philosophy is a reaffirmation of Dewey's, although he is considerably more articulate. There is the same rejection of metaphysics and theology. There is the same insistence that the origin of social problems concerns happenings within the sphere of natural experience alone and that their solutions have to be found by using the instrumentalities of method alone. There is also the assertion that all the meanings associated with human existence derive from experience in the natural order, that one does not have to look beyond life on this planet for direction concerning the means to happiness in temporal existence. Nagel's position on moral theory is practically a restatement of Dewey's. "If moral problems can be resolved at all, they can be resolved only in the light of specific human capacities, historical circumstances and acquired skills, and the opportunities . . . for altering the physical and social environment and for redirecting habitual behaviors." [33]

The fundamental position and goal of naturalism as defined by Ernest Nagel is that:

It holds that the world consists of the coming to be and passing away of substantial things, that there is a discoverable order in their rise, continuance and decay, and

---

curs is a phase in a unitary, teleologically organized, and all-inclusive process of system" (*Ibid.*, p. 8). One question which one could now ask is, What is this "positive evidence?" No mention is made in this work what this positive evidence consists of. A second question is, How could there be concrete evidence which would be actually *negative* to the idea of teleology unless it embraced *all* of the facts of the cosmos in their modes of interrelationship and unless the investigator is prepared to show that these are in no way a support for each other. At any time that one form of being incorporates another within itself without becoming subject to the determinate and *determining* structure of the other, there is a case of teleological support, whether there is any cosmic consciousness of it or not.

[33] *Ibid.*, p. 11.

that nature is completely intelligible in terms of their determinate characters, so that the alleged operation of disembodied forms is not relevant to nature's order or to our knowledge of it.[34]

But is nature completely intelligible in terms of any set of knowable entities which are within the reach of human understanding? If this were true then it should be possible to induce life artificially in nonliving matter. If there are no such things as disembodied forms, or forms present substantially in matter, it should be possible to provoke life into matter in its most elemental structures. The fact that this has not yet been done does not, of course, mean that the naturalist philosophers are incorrect. But Nagel's assumption regarding the existential causal primacy of matter in the executive order of nature ought to be carefully examined. If he means that material processes and these alone are the sole explanation for the entire existential order, including the work of reason and consciousness, then the only difference between his naturalist viewpoint and that of Friedrich Engels is the inner dialectic of matter in the case of the latter. That is, there is no evolutionary historicism associated with naturalist materialism. There is just an acceptance of matter as the primary cause of nature in its immediate sense. There is no inquiry about what brought the order of nature to its present state, and no concern for its evolutionary outcome.

What is the position of naturalist philosophy regarding man's own particular role in the existential order? Dewey and Nagel both reject any teleological idea about existential goals grounded in man's nature because teleological connections are not empirically verifiable. They point out that there is no evidence pointing to any cosmic concern over what man's lot on earth is. But it is the term "concern" which seems to con-

---

[34] *Ibid.*, p. 40.

fuse the issue here, particularly insofar as Dewey and Nagel apparently refer to it in a strictly anthropomorphic sense. The teleological question is whether or not the whole existential order includes the conditions requisite for the evolvement of higher forms out of lower ones and the dependence of the former upon the latter, even while higher forms operate on higher levels of novelty and freedom. It is not a matter of whether atomic particles are subjectively "interested" in sustaining human life. The question is whether or not these particles sustain it, and if they do, how this structure is arranged.

What seems to be a main characteristic of naturalism is its preoccupation with the method of thinking—the problem of analysis. "Its task is analytical and critical," Nagel writes. "It studies the meaning and structure of statements, discovers what pervasive characters nature owns, and so determines the conditions for intelligible discourse and rational practice. The task of philosophy can be briefly defined as the analysis of categories." [35] This definition, however, Nagel adds, can be taken only with the stipulation that the meaning of a category is to be clarified by reference to its linguistic usage as it is applied to determinate and identifiable subject matter. "The validity of a categorial analysis," he says, "is at all times an empirical matter." [36]

There are some points which need to be clarified. One is that there is a recurrence of the old problem of the category and the determinateness of existents. Aristotle hurdled this problem with his assumption that the categories refer to the way things actually exist. However, he seemed to have overlooked the fact that one has no way of encountering things intellectually except by way of the categories which are formed by the mind. The conformance between the nature of the object and the categories through which the object is intellectu-

[35] Ibid., p. 41.
[36] Ibid., p. 41.

ally apprehended is only supposed. One is never able to step outside of one's conceptualized schema of consciousness and actually measure the conformance between this schema and the real nature of what is thus encountered. Subject matter becomes determinate and identifiable only through the use of constructs of the mind. It is by use of these that one approaches, conceptually, the world of appearances. Even the term *empirical* is a rational category. The term denotes a close alliance of conceptual and perceptual faculties—one which permits no deviation in content from one to the other. But the alliance—that which is the very root of the empirical idea—is not effused out of bare perception. It is, on the contrary, expressed through the idea of *relation* which is, in turn, a category of the mind.

One fact which ought to be faced constantly is that there is a gap between sensory perception and the concepts which correspondingly arise which neither science nor philosophy has been able to close. Even the mighty Kant, after having meticulously and carefully arrived at a metaphysical deduction of the category and a transcendental deduction of judgments, concluded that the issue was hopelessly far from any real solution. According to Nagel, naturalist philosophers "cannot reject sense and intellect as incompatible poles of human activity." [37] Since sense and intellect are conjoined in the act of producing knowledge, one could hardly do other than agree with him on this point. But while they may not be incompatible, they are poles apart as far as any genuine synthesis is concerned. Accordingly, one ought to weigh carefully the following comment:

> Stable knowledge is there equated neither with sensation nor with an original intuition into a realm of pure meanings. On the contrary, it is acquired through the use of

[37] *Ibid.*, p. 41.

general ideas suggested by traits of empirical subject matter, which are dialectically elaborated and supported by evidence secured through the senses.[38]

Granted, stable knowledge is not to be equated with sensation, for sensation is merely unreflected experience. Also, it cannot be assumed that it is an original intuition into the realm of pure meaning, for one has no certain knowledge what pure meanings are or where they may be found. General ideas are the original forms from which knowledge emerges, stable or otherwise. But one may have some reservations about Nagel's saying that general ideas are "suggested by traits of empirical subject matter." If the trait which is to be found is located in the empirical subject matter then there is no real suggesting, for subject matter does not suggest—it does not even speak. It is man who does the speaking and the suggesting, and he does it through his power of reflective synthesis. As for the latter part, "dialectically elaborated and supported by evidence secured through the senses," what does the dialectical elaborating? Is this done by sense evidence? Is this a lapse into Locke's procedure of tracing the generation of an idea to an isomorphic origin of it in sensation? The support of sensation is certainly admissible insofar as sensation supplies short-range confirmation of simple properties. But dialectical elaboration, or for that matter any elaboration, does not occur through sense experience. While there may be no original intuition in the realm of pure meanings, there is, nonetheless, the corrective work of the intellect assimilating, separating, comparing and rejecting that which does not fit into the logical synthesis which it constructs as its own rule.

In addition to supporting as its main task the analysis of categories, naturalist philosophers also profess a position of undisputed supremacy of existential subject matter. "In the procedure of the sciences," says Nagel, "a rationalist empiri-

---

[38] *Ibid.*, p. 43.

cism exhibits in a most profound form the union of intellect and sense." [39] This is seldom questioned by anyone. It is quite compatible in any philosophy to have a systematic evaluation of the way that related propositions touch upon each other, and philosophers also tend to accept the existential order as real. One can easily grant that empirical science is an example of the close compatibility of intellect and sense. But sense and intellect are still wide apart. If the true function of philosophy is the analysis of categories, and of science the discovery of the conditions for the occurrences of events, there is still left unanswered the problem of how events which are extra-mental translate themselves into conceptualized categorial forms.

One is at a loss, for example, to know what is meant by "empirical" subject matter. If it is matter "for a subject," then it must be in a form which is in accord with the mode of the receiver. The response of a dog could hardly be expected to be the same as that of a man when both are confronted with the same phenomenon. While a man may scrutinize in detail a new phenomenon, a dog may do nothing more than look at it and wag his tail. If subject matter means precisely the kind of appearance which can be received by a subject, then the term *empirical* is simply an accessory fact, having really nothing to do with subject matter reception. On the other hand, if "empirical subject matter" derives its meaning from the sole fact that there is a material object capable of being perceived by a person, there is nothing which would indicate how or in what way this subject matter is received.

The main point about subject matter is that it is something to be expressed in a syntactical order. Nagel writes: "For it is the structure of subject matter which determines the relevance and truth of our discourse about it; and one of the tasks of philosophy is to exhibit this fact. Purely dialectical

---

[39] *Ibid.*, p. 45.

considerations are therefore never sufficient to resolve problems arising from the study of nature." [40] If the whole of naturalist philosophy is a concern for dialectical argument and the empirical data of nature, then it is obviously the latter that one must turn to for determining the relevance and truth of the discourse about it. But then the discourse is perhaps circular. How can the very thing which one is trying to understand determine what is relevant to understanding it?

There is, however, a recognition of this problem in naturalist philosophy. There is a clear indication in Nagel's case that inferential principles are not assumed to have traits in common with mechanisms present in the subject matter. Naturalist logic is not grounded in the idea that rational operations grow out of biological and physical ones. "Suggestions for inferential canons," Nagel says, "may indeed be obtained from observations of natural processes; but the fact that a principle may have been suggested in this way does not explain its normative function." [41]

What is the naturalist contribution to the problem of man in society? Part of the development of the naturalist method can be seen in the works of two eminent philosophers. In both cases the point was stressed that philosophy can be of service only when the problem cases require remedial action. Dewey especially called attention to the problems arising in the twentieth century from a conflict of personal interests and those of institutions having inherited incompatible tendencies. But naturalist philosophers have done little to answer this problem because they have gone further in the direction of a solution than merely to point out the problem. Man's intelligence is not an infallible instrument, but it is the only rational instrument which he has. It has been pointed out in the works of both Dewey and Nagel that supplication to an unseen power

[40] Ibid., p. 44.
[41] Ibid., p. 78.

does not remove the natural deficiencies in man's way of existing. But these do not seem to be removable by the sheer force of a sharpened logic either. Is there something in man's behavior which is an actual force of unification; something which philosophers have overlooked?

In Dewey's *Reconstruction* one looks in vain for a new guide to moral behavior. In the works of Nagel there is considerable emphasis on the technique of empirical investigation and categorial analysis. There is also a great stress upon the use of intelligence in the making of decisions. But a concentration of speculation on the use of method alone leads nowhere as far as decisional matters concerning man's interior motives are concerned. The human psyche cannot be corralled in this way. Logic is a lure for it, but it is only a lure; it is not a compelling force. In every case there is an encounter with man's freedom which is not a pure spontaneity but the liberty of an interior core of selfhood which has always been far too elusive for the rather coarse methods of empirical study.

One would certainly not wish to contest the idea of reason in behavior. But, what makes a moral or a social act intelligent? One can act intelligently in matters pertaining to science because there is, first of all, *a* science to be intelligent about. One can be intelligent in the use of linguistic symbols only because there is first of all *a* language and *a* set of rules regarding its use. How then, can one act *intelligently* about social matters without a set of normative rules regarding what is correct in man's performance in the social situation?

There is no denying that the emphasis of naturalist philosophy on methodology is important. But the naturalist philosophers whose works have been discussed seem to be hesitant to go in any direction other than an excursion into methodology. But if it is man's reason which recognizes the requirements of methodology, it is also man's reason which recognizes the concepts of logical necessity. The idea of *cause*, whether material or formal, is certainly impressed upon the human mind with the same force as any hypothesis concerning the use of categories. For the categories pertain not just to abstract notions of inference, but to real, empirical things.

There does not appear to be any detached way for a philosophy to take all of the existential data into account, for man as individual subjectivity is indeed a part of the whole structure. He must try to assess and to understand all which is about him, not merely what is outward and external but also what is inward and subjective. Animals do not gather information and write about their experiences, but humans do. From the very dawn of consciousness in man, and with the development of an articulate language, man has expressed himself in an ever-widening expanse of culture. What seems to be a perennial fact of human nature is that it expresses itself reflectively. It reveals itself in all its joys and sufferings, in its heights of exultation and its depths of sorrow. Moreover, it reveals itself in its inner mode of grasping what is beyond the reach of sense. The intellect is a powerful instrument which has managed to conquer much of the world of fact. But this is true only because it has not been bound in its activity to the limited causal situations in which the world of physical fact is given.

CHAPTER III

The Existentialist Answer

MARCEL'S *ONTOLOGICAL MYSTERY*

WHAT QUALIFIES MARCEL as an existentialist, if nothing else, is that for him the focus of philosophy is the flux of events in which one incessantly finds himself—events which threaten always to become terminal and meaningless.

Not for a moment does Marcel question the existence of the soul. On the surface of existence there is that overwhelming actuality of an *I* which thinks; an *I* which has a body, an *I* which also tries to comprehend the ontological presence of being. This *I* is far more than what is exposed in Descartes' *Cogito*, which is an *I* that is a subject for cognizing objective reality. Marcel's *I* is one which is a part of the unfathomable mystery of being. It is an *I* which exists, but whose existence transcends the set of determinable causes which have a certain displacement in the world of physical facts. The *I* in this case is one which has been transported into a region of being which is outside concrete physical determination, for it is an *I* which managed to discover itself. In this act it is an ineffable mystery. It is not that mankind cannot solve the ontological mystery of being which bothers Marcel, but rather that man has not even a perfunctory interest in the mystery itself. "The characteristic feature of the age," he wrote, "seems to be what might be called the misplacement of the idea of function, taking function in its current sense, which includes both the vital and social functions." [1]

Man has, in other words, ceased to regard himself in any way other than as an aggregate of functions which have to be tended to. But in reducing himself to this, he loses at the same time a sense of meaning. The *I* disappears in the satisfaction of the body and the ego. Functions are proper to all, and all have the same functions. What more abrupt way is there for man to lose his whole sense of personal identity—his awareness of a deeply personal *I*—than by dissolving his whole being in what is never individually but only collectively true?

> Surely everything both within and outside of him conspires to identify this man with his functions—meaning not only with his functions as worker, as trade-union member, or as voter, but with his vital functions as well. The rather horrible expression "time-table" perfectly describes his life.[2]

This is, no doubt, a part of the price which has to be paid for the external comforts of urban civilization. A society created by technology cannot avoid becoming in some sense what it has created. It adopts the methods and the outcomes of technology as an expression of its own inner logic. It cannot abstain from being somewhat mirrored in its own devices. It must, therefore, accept its inherent pattern of living as something which is socially inescapable. What there is of a common philosophy seldom penetrates the external crust of socialized man in order to enter the meaning of being. Man is far too preoccupied with having to execute the mundane details of

---

[1] Gabriel Marcel, *The Philosophy of Existentialism*, tr. Manya Harari (London: The Harvill Press, 1948), p. 10.
[2] *Ibid.*, p. 11.

existence and with having to pretend to be happy and contented with the result. "But," says Marcel,

> besides the sadness felt by the onlooker, there is the dull, intolerable unease felt by the actor himself who is reduced to living as though he were in fact submerged by his functions. This uneasiness is enough to show that there is in all this some appalling mistake, some ghastly misunderstanding, implanted in defenseless minds by an increasingly inhuman philosophy (for if the philosophy has prepared the way for the order, the order has also shaped philosophy).[3]

What purports to pass for philosophy is, in effect, not philosophy at all but a pseudo-technology of personal existence. Rather than bringing to a level of consciousness the inner workings of the order of existence, this pseudotechnology only incurs a deeper morass of problems with which this new social science is in no way competent to deal. Despite the efforts of what Marcel calls a "degraded rationalism," there is no total accounting in terms of cause-effect relationships for more than a small fraction of what one encounters. "And in addition to these theoretical puzzles," he wrote, "there are innumerable technical problems, bound up with the difficulty of knowing how the various functions, once they have been inventoried and labelled, can be made to work together without doing one another harm."

The "ontological need" of which Marcel speaks is something unique in his work—something which has no place in naturalist logic. For one thing it does not concern the method of analysis, but it does concern the one who analyzes. It is a need for affirmation—an affirmation which answers the question "Who am I?" and in doing so is able to answer the ques-

---

[3] *Ibid.,* p. 12.

tion of being in its entirety. The subject "who" is intrinsically bound up in the predicate *I* so that an ontological separation is never possible. It does not simply raise the question of Descartes' *"Cogito"*—of the existence of a thinking subject. What is raised here is the double question of whether there is *being,* and whether the *I* is part of it. This is, ironically, a question which one is not even able to raise until one has answered it.

The ontological need is certainly there as one becomes aware of it in noting the fact of *presence.* But beyond this, Marcel suspects that the characteristic of this need can never be wholly clear to oneself.

> Being is—or should be—necessary. It is impossible that everything should be reduced to a play of successive appearances which are inconsistent with each other ("inconsistent" is essential), or in the words of Shakespeare, to "a tale told by an idiot." [4]

Even pessimism attends to this need for presence. Having the appearance of negation is, on its reverse side, an affirmation that *being* ought to be where it is not. Philosophy which refrains from endorsing the ontological need does so only by ignoring it. But those who do ignore the personal in all its forms, reducing it to its caricatural expressions, also distort its essential character. Marcel believes, however, that mutilating the life of the spirit at its root will never silence the ontological need. Even though contemporary philosophy may be mainly sidetracked with concern over verification, the ontological mystery still abides; if not to reveal itself completely, to be at least implicit in the reality of presence through love which "infinitely transcends all possible verification because it exists in an immediacy beyond all conceivable mediation." [5]

---

[4] *Ibid.,* p. 14.
[5] *Ibid.,* p. 15.

The ontological problem is mainly this: to inquire into the mystery of being one must oppose oneself as subject to what one supposes to be objectively represented, but in doing so the mystery disappears in that *being* now becomes a problem, but unfortunately that kind of problem in which being is in search of something less than itself. Marcel asks, "How am I qualified to begin this investigation?"[6] In this case Descartes' *Cogito* does not help at all, for the only certainty which it can provide is one of the person as a subject of objective cognition. Surely cognition is being, but not in a complete and full sense. It does not take into account the need for cognition, but only the act itself, in which the being of the inquiring subject is presupposed but never acted on. It is certainly legitimate, he says, to try to raise certain distinctions within the unity of the one who thinks and who also tries to *think himself,* but one must be able to go beyond such distinctions in order that the ontological problem can arise. The problem, when it does arise, must then relate to that *being* in respect to his all-comprehensive unity. "To sum up our reflections at this point," Marcel says, "we find that we are dealing with an urge toward an affirmation—yet an affirmation which it seems impossible to make, since it is not until it has been made that I can regard myself as qualified to make it." [7]

There are two questions which ought to be raised and answered in order to locate a new point of orientation in Marcel's thinking. One is the meaning of mystery; the other is how love gives some insight into the ontological need and the mystery associated with it. About the first, Marcel says that "A mystery is a problem which encroaches upon its own data, invading them, as it were, and thereby transcending itself as a simple problem." [8] There is, for example, a mystery in the

---

6 *Ibid.,* p. 16.
7 *Ibid.,* p. 17.
8 *Ibid.,* p. 19.

expression "I have a body," for the *I* cannot become separate from the body which the *I* claims that it has. Similarly, there is a mystery of evil; for evil, insofar as it is cognitively recognized, is something problematic. This is not the same as when the *I* experiences evil as a deprivation of its own being. Love conquers in some way the distinction between what is in one and what is before one in that the love act is an affirmation of being which not only affirms itself but also that which is loved. Love is the starting point for understanding such mysteries as those of body and soul. But because it is itself enveloped in mystery, one cannot ask for the criteria of true love. Criteria can be asked for only in the domain of the objective and the problematical.

Although one speaks of the ontological problem which is concerned with the mystery of being, the mystery is itself in the realm of the meta-problematic. That is, it is beyond the level of the ordinary problematic because it is something which cannot be understood in terms of a content of thought. According to Marcel, "Content is . . . derived from experience, whereas it is only by way of liberation and detachment from experience that we can possibly rise to the level of the meta-problematical and of mystery." [9] Love momentarily transcends the problematic in that it is purely and simply a need of *being* being asserted. But there are other kinds of human experience which likewise point to *being* in its moments of self-affirmation. There is, for example, recollection, which Marcel regards as a "re-collecting" of oneself as a unity. In this act, one transcends the old dualism of being and action, for the action is indeed toward *being* in the immediate sense. This, Marcel insists, is not the *für sich sein,* the "for itself," which is the central theme of German Idealism. This is no case of abstract *being* in which the human experiences of despair and of fear

---

[9] *Ibid.,* p. 23.

are reduced to some momentary reflexes of the Absolute. Recollection, as Marcel uses the term, is an actual recognizance of *being* in which all its tragic factors are united in such a way that the positive self-affirmation of *being* can oppose what is negative to it. Only through despair, for example, can hope arise, for although hope may be seen as animating the optimism of technical progress, the only genuine hope is that which does not spring from one's achievements; it is hope which springs from humility rather than from pride. For Marcel, hope is not some "listless waiting." "Hope," he says,

> consists in asserting that there is at the heart of being, beyond all data, beyond all inventories and all calculations, a mysterious principle which is in connivance with me, which cannot but will that which I will, if what I will deserves to be willed and is, in fact, willed by the whole of my being.[10]

In this case Marcel seems to be utilizing the principle of a prayerful attitude in man in accordance with the idea of "Thy will be done." It is that kind of hope in which man as individual subverts his entire being to the Being of God in the possible expectation that the wills in both cases coincide. In this case the mystery asserts itself in a most profound sense, for it is set against the problematical. Hope in this case is not that sort of optimism which assumes that scientific intelligence can relieve man of the conflicts inherent in social existence. It makes no pretense of any easing of the difficulties of such existence because it is founded on an admission that the ontological mystery permits of no easy resolving of the deeper movements of personality as these are set in a technologically oriented civilization. "Every technique," says Marcel,

---

[10] *Ibid.*, p. 28.

serves or can be made to serve, some desire or some fear; conversely every desire, as every fear, tends to invent its appropriate technique. From this standpoint, despair consists in the recognition of the ultimate inefficacy of all technics, joined to the inability of the refusal to change over to a new ground—a ground where all techniques are seen to be incompatible with the fundamental nature of being, which itself escapes our grasp (in so far as our grasp is limited to the world of objects and to this alone). ... To the question: What can man achieve? we continue to reply: He can achieve as much as his technics; yet we are obliged to admit that these technics are unable *to save man himself,* and even that they are apt to conclude the most sinister alliance with the enemy he bears within him.[11]

The enemy of which Marcel speaks is no sinister demon —no "spiritus malignus" implanted in human nature to connive to defeat man by some diabolical scheme which would turn his techniques against him. Man is at the mercy of these techniques, but he still controls them. What the problem is resides in controlling the control. What is lacking in one sense is a precise knowledge of what should be controlled and how. What is at stake is not just the physical competence and the psychological satisfaction of man but rather the contentment of a tranquil soul. Despair seems to be inevitable, but it need not be regarded as man's natural condition. It grows out of the mind's reaching toward that which it can never attain. "The more the sense of the ontological tends to disappear," Marcel wrote, "the more unlimited becomes the claim of the mind which has lost it to a kind of cosmic governance, because it is less and less capable of examining its own credentials to the exercise of such dominion." [12]

---

[11] *Ibid.,* p. 30.
[12] *Ibid.,* p. 31.

The way out, it seems, is a restructuring of man in his experience, a rescuing of man through hope. The objection will be raised, of course, that this is no more than a disquieting kind of moralism which merely invites submission or inert passivity. But Marcel is careful to guard against this sort of implication. Hope is the activity of the will when it is made to bear on what it is not itself. It is a transfer of the object of will so that there is no longer a stiffening of the soul—no continual falling back on self. What does one find in this humble withdrawal? No less than all, for in this relaxation it once again becomes creative. "Where there is creation there is no degradation. . . . Degradation begins at the point where creativeness falls into self-limitation." [13]

From what does creativity spring? For one thing, from fidelity—faithfulness to a principle. It is a faithful adherence to what can be maintained in and before one as presence. A person is a reality which is more than object. It is a kind of influx which requires one to be permeable to it, not to command it—but to call it forth. But this notion of influx can be accepted only at the "meta-problematical level." It must be handled as an expression of being, or presence. No claims are made here for the reawakening of the human spirit toward the pursuit of the ontological mystery as far as social mechanisms are concerned. The focus is not on a rejuvenated society but on man. All that can be expected is a softening of the blows of circumstances through a rekindling of a new attitude toward tragedy. It is a fact that the bonds of humanity are knit through by that influx of presence which is the gift of self to another.

It is the mystery itself which concerns Marcel more than what ultimate results might occur out of resolving it. It is not a mystery which is required to be solved, but rather one which

---

[13] *Ibid.,* p. 33.

needs to be understood as existing. For so long as the soul is given over completely to the world of the problematical its capacity to hope diminishes. Insofar as it is continually chained to experience, the soul faces nothing but despair. On the other hand, the soul which is at the disposal of others—the one which knows that it is not its own but it is inwardly consecrated and dedicated—conveys itself readily as presence. To Marcel, hope, presence, and creative fidelity are the marks by which one reconstructs actions and attitudes which conform to the fullness of being made explicit in the Incarnation of Christ. Presence is conveyed in the Eucharist, whereas creative fidelity becomes explicit in the work of the Church. But here Marcel recognizes that these marks do not carry that sort of meaning for those who ignore Christianity or for those who refuse to accept it. In answer to what may be a possible objection, he says that "Christian data may be necessary *in fact* to enable the mind to conceive some of the notions which I have attempted to analyze; but these notions cannot be said to depend on the data of Christianity, and they do not presuppose it." [14]

The philosopher is now in that historical situation where he cannot avoid acknowledging even that which he tends to reject. While the truth of the Christian religion may be taken as either true or false, the situation implies the existence of the Christian fact so that one can no more ignore positive science. The role in either case is no more than that of a fertilizing principle. That is, because of Christianity, as in the case of positive science, certain ideas have developed which could not have been conceived without it.

JASPERS' *REASON AND EXISTENZ*

In the view of Karl Jaspers, contemporary philosophy was born in the works of two European philosophers, Nietzsche

---
[14] *Ibid.*, p. 44.

and Kierkegaard. A reverse reaction to the optimistic rationalism which had so largely dominated philosophy in the eighteenth century could well have been expected. But who expected, who anticipated that the unrational could take its place? Yet this is what happened. It was the unrational which was central in the philosophy of world recurrence in Nietzsche and in the Christological negation of this world in Kierkegaard.

Both men seemed to have been drawn by an overwhelming awe of Being—that totality of existence of which man can have but a small glimpse, even though he tries by it to construct his own rational order. The purpose of philosophy for Nietzsche and that of philosophical theology for Kierkegaard were somewhat identical: to open men's eyes to the utter smallness of their vision; to show to what paradoxical positions one could be led once the hold of empirical exactness is shaken loose. The unrational in their positions is not simply that of a hostility to reason, but rather their openness to a new intellectual attitude in which an utter faith in scientific knowledge is a form of naiveté. Men who place their faith totally in science have not, according to Nietzsche's and Kierkegaard's ways of thinking, reached that critical point in maturity when one understands more and more that there are things which one cannot understand.

Although late in receiving recognition, the work of each man provided in its own way the keystone of the contemporary existentialist endeavor to "push into the widest range of the possible." For Jaspers, this "widest range of the possible" is an Encompassing All which envelops not only that which has been given existence but also Being as it can concern the "self-supporting ground of Being, whether it is Being in itself or Being as it is for us." [15]

---

[15] Karl Jaspers, *Reason and Existenz*, tr. William Earle (New York: The Noonday Press, 1955), p. 52.

Jaspers chose the term *Encompassing* as something to which one must fix his mind to apprehend the true and complete significance of Being. One's concept of Being fades away as soon as one tries to establish it in any determinate way. Apprehension must take place according to the modes in which Being can be entertained as a concept. The customary way of regarding it is empirically in terms of what is given in the phenomenal area of Nature, World, or God. Empirical existence is an overpowering Other which is the ground and material cause of one's own being. But as cause it is not something entirely apart. One is also Being in other modes as well. One is given in the Encompassing in a fuller sense than as being merely determined.

A second mode of the Encompassing is consciousness as such. "Only what appears to our consciousness as experienceable, as an object, has being for us." [16] Being is not just given as determining, but also as determinable, as becoming an object for conscious reflection.

Two meanings are assigned to consciousness. For one thing it is conscious living existence, but not yet encompassing. One is bound by it in several places; as a collection of beings living consciously, and then as a corporate consciousness as such. That is, man is a whole of that which is consciousness taken in its entirety. As Jaspers states, "We participate not only in the validity of knowledge, but also in a universally recognizable formal lawfulness in willing, action and feeling." [17]

But these two, empirical existence and consciousness, do not exhaust what is given in the Encompassing. There is yet another mode, Spirit, which Jaspers says is "a totality of intelligible thought, action and feeling—a totality which is not a closed object for knowledge but remains Idea." [18] The ne-

---

16 *Ibid.*, p. 55.
17 *Ibid.*, p. 57.
18 *Ibid.*, p. 65.

cessity for Spirit as another mode of the Encompassing is given in the fact that the empirical world is continually falling apart and continually being reconstructed in new totalities. Like empirical existence, spirit is a temporal process, but it is marked by the reflexivity of knowledge rather than by biological or psychological processes. These several modes do not imply separate facts about the Encompassing, but rather separate starting points. The second, consciousness, is not something independent—it points to its basis in empirical existence, but on the other side it points to spirit—to the power which it must let itself be dominated by if it is to have a real meaning and totality.

So far the Encompassing is something abstract; it is only possibility. All its modes can be regarded in terms of potential. It is simply Being in transcendence standing over against empirical existence as if nothing were revealed. It is through Existence that Being becomes certain, that it becomes knowing, known and knowable. Even transcendence is unfathomable except through the Media of Existence without which Being is a vast desert. "Existence, although never itself becoming an object or form, carries the meaning of every mode of the Encompassing." [19] In itself Existenz is an object of no science; it cannot be revealed in itself anywhere or in anything. It is a counterpart of Spirit in that it never moves to be whole. It breaks up any whole, while never reaching any totality itself. "It is then," Jaspers says,

> what goes beyond all limits, the omnipresent demand of thought that not only grasps what is universal value and is the *ens rationes* in the sense of being a law or principle of order of some process, but also brings to light the Other, stands before the absolutely counter-rational, touching it and bringing it, too, into being.[20]

[19] *Ibid.*, p. 67.
[20] *Ibid.*, p. 65.

There are two sides of human existence which, in every mode of the Encompassing, encounter one another. Without existence, reason would be a futile gesture having no determinate content. Without reason, existence would fade into darkness. Each is oriented toward the other; reason toward control of Existence which supports it, and Existence to Transcendence through which it first became an independent cause. "Without Transcendence, Existenz becomes a sterile loveless and demoniac defiance . . . without reason, Existenz is inactive, sleeping and as though not there." [21]

Having now set up the Encompassing according to its modes and to the way in which these modes are related to each other, Jaspers proceeds next to draw out the ways in which it becomes operative in human activity. The Encompassing cannot be understood like some object in the world. If one acquires it as thought, it could be derived only from that which can be thought of. If one regards it as consciousness, it could not be derived from anything which appears to consciousness. Similarly it cannot be empirical existence, for then it could not be derived from any objectively known thing. But it does order the set of all its modes, and it does become an apparent object for all systematic disciplines of investigation. It is through it that anthropology, psychology, and the humanist science sociology become possible and have their contents. In contrast to the situation of animals who are unaware of their biological order and who have no historical identity with other examples of their own species, man, while exercising greater individual detachment than animals, is far more conditioned by the fact of community which, in his case, is far different from animal collectives. "His community," says Jaspers, "is first of all, no state of immediacy, but is mediated through a relation to common conscious purposes in the world, through a relation to truth, and through relation to God." [22] It is moved

---

[21] *Ibid.*, p. 67.
[22] *Ibid.*, p. 78.

constantly in relation to changing potential contents which are, in effect, a continual unfolding of what is gathered out of the past and present. Human nature is determined as a matter of tradition as well as heredity. Truth—the truth of the human situation as produced in and through the Encompassing—cannot be separate from communication. It is by way of this that reason unites the fragmented fact into a coherent whole. But reason is not a lawless power. It is bound by a system of rules which is its own. Reason rules, but the rule of reason itself is logic.

TRUTH AS COMMUNICABILITY

Having acquired some understanding of the modes of the Encompassing one can now proceed to make a further elaboration of the function of truth along definite lines of contemplation. The main concern consists of trying to discern the ways in which truth is related to the human situation, for it is both in the revealing and in the revealed that truth is recognized for what it is.

The human situation is different from that of animals in the respect that man's role is far more than a biological one. Animal community is determined by relatively few elements of companionship as compared with that of man.

The idiom "Truth as Communicability" does not imply that error can appear as truth simply because it is communicated. What is rather the case is that it assumes a variety of shapes because there is a variety of means of communication. "For what truth is," Jaspers says,

> is determined by the character of the Encompassing within which communication takes place; for example, communication from one empirical existent to another, or in consciousness as such, or in the idea of spirit; and then further, it is determined by whether it is achieved in the

binding together of those modes of the Encompassing in reason and its basis, Existenz.[23]

One observes the meaning of truth as it is derived in each of the several modes. These differ both in relation to the particular need which is sought, and to the kind of relationship in which the empirical self finds itself with respect to the Encompassing. Being appears and is expressed under each mode—but the being of self is likewise stratified in the same manner and the reaction is determined by each of the respective strata.

Empirical existence involves the will to preserve and develop itself indefinitely. But again, man does not achieve this by himself, but through the community. Need binds all together in a common defense against nature. Private interests alone stand out in a sort of tension toward the common bond, ready to break out when the need slackens. There is always an "unsocial sociability" threatening to dissolve the bond. Danger, however, forces each to recognize what is necessary, and the greater the danger the more decisive is the will to unite. It is resident in what emerges and comes to pass.

Truth as consciousness is something else. It is a capacity for cogent correctness. It is truth by which in logical categories one can grasp what is true and valid for everyone. "It is the truth of a self-identical consciousness dispersed into the multiplicity of its empirical existence." [24] It is a truth which flows easily from one empiricist consciousness to another, carried on the solid ground of logic which conveys without loss of content. As it appears through the communication of spirit, truth is the Idea as reflecting its communal substance. The regular empirical existence falls away in this which is the

---

23 *Ibid.*, p. 80.
24 *Ibid.*, p. 82.

totality of human achievement expressed in terms of its denominate ideals and characteristics.

Now, while it is the usefulness of consequences for actions and the timeless rightness of what is universally valid "which are the marks of truth" in the first two modes of the Encompassing, what comes in the third—that of Spirit—is communication. It is no longer sufficient here that one is able to apply the categories to comprehend empirical existence and to establish once and for all a rule of thought. "Who speaks and understands here speaks out of the substance of an Idea." [25]

While truth-seeking plays a role in each of the modes, there is yet no indication of what truth really is. In each there is a certain insufficiency which is revealed in the fact that truth cannot become completely intelligible in any case. Empirical existence, for example, seeks gratification—happiness; but the content of happiness is never clear. If one were ever to secure perfect contentment, this would destroy him. His will, which often seeks without knowing what it is which it seeks, would be forever silenced.

What happens when truth in any mode of the Encompassing is absolutized? Jaspers says that when natural existence is taken for the sole fact of Being there is a surrender of both the valid truths of consciousness and of the Idea of Spirit. Scientific analysis can always wring out of experience a certain number of salient facts and recognizable regularities so that men tend toward a complete reliance on the methods and the findings of science. "The essence of man," Jaspers says,

> is lost in this blind reliance upon nature, where his existence seems identical with nature and nature identical with knowable regularities. For even if those regularities or laws were exhaustively known, they could only make mat-

[25] Ibid., p. 84.

ter and biological life comprehensible, not man—only man is a species of animals which could then be endangered, the sick animal.[26]

When attention is given only to the matter of here-and-now existence, there is the possibility of man's lapsing into that type of animal existence which is sustained, like that of ants, through preserving a technical apparatus. It would be a self-repeating, but non-historical species of living things; like an astonishing but now forgotten movement in humanity. It could last for a long time, but with a thorough change in the living conditions of the earth, final catastrophe would come to this species.

Absolutizing each of the other modes of the Encompassing leads to similar results. Where thinking in consciousness as such is interested in its own self-sufficiency "it is taking its timeless validities as absolute, as though the truth and Being itself were thereby grasped, as though it had read off the order and laws of things beyond all relativity." [27] On the other hand, absolutizing of Spirit amounts to a similar situation in thinking which creates a hollow world. All of these modes must be perceived in order to contain their interconnectedness. The lower level must be limited to contain the possibility of the higher, whereas the higher cannot be actualized in isolation. From the standpoint of sheer existents, lower ones can stand without the higher, whereas the converse is not true. But this is not authentic existence. "Man can endure," writes Jaspers, "as a living existent, but he ceased to be a man, just as every being can die, and dead matter have the victorious durations." [28]

Even though there may be a whole new way of looking at

---

[26] *Ibid.,* p. 87.
[27] *Ibid.,* p. 88.
[28] *Ibid.,* p. 90.

things, one is yet unsatisfied; and what is decisively unsatisfactory is the fact that the modes of the Encompassing do not themselves tend to a unified, self-completed whole. For this will to grasp the three modes together and to experience the impossibility of any real synthesis grows out of something which cannot be found in any one of the modes, nor in the three of them taken together. The will to communicate in the several of them "holds its own energy at the service of a universal will to communicate which comes out of reason and Existenz." [29]

Although the communication of Existenz is carried out by way of membership in the spirit utilizing and thereby affirming universal consciousness and empirical fact, it is expressly done by those who push on through these to *will to become themselves*. In contrast to that sort of struggle which involves power and superiority, this is a struggle in which every advance of the whole, and every destruction is similarly total, Jaspers speaks here of a "crack in Being," a glinting through empirical fact which is a moment of the imminence of Being in us which opens the way for transcendence. *Here is the way for fully authentic living—to be in communication unconditionally by losing one's self completely.* What is authentically human is not a collection of individual examples binding themselves together. Communication produces also that which is communicating—independent natures coming to consciousness of themselves as if bound eternally to do so. While it is reason which penetrates everything, "Existenz as the ground bears in its depths the organ which is present in all modes of the Encompassing which is the universal bond as well as the unrest which disturbs every fixation." [30]

Is there a meaning of truth which can be said to be in some sense final? There is, Jaspers says, a will to total communica-

29 *Ibid.*, p. 91.
30 *Ibid.*, p. 92.

tion which is also the authentically driving and binding force in all modes of communication. But this will does not itself reach fulfillment. It is limited through its own historicity and through that of the three modes. Truth, then, can only *become*. Out of the radical openness of the will to communicate, truth is always partially revealed and partially achieved. How far can it be ever revealed in time? In answering this, Jaspers takes truth in its double sense of dogmatic and communicative. When it is grasped conclusively in object, symbol and experiencing, it is closed in itself, complete and independent of man. Truth as dogmatic is something to which men refer but in which they do not themselves participate. When it would finally bind itself to communication it would be different. It would arise and actualize only through the act of communication; it would not be valid except through this. This is not something which can be secured and kept through disciplinary exercise. There is, Jaspers says, that kind of truth which is reached by restriction to rationally clear ends. But this, he insists, has accomplished little in historical communication. What is required is a bringing forth of humanity under conditions of communication which are limitlessly clarifying—by that in which truth is persistently revealing itself. Herein lies the radical difference between dogmatic and communicative truths—a difference between that which is discovered and that which is produced. What he seems to set down as the ground of all truth is that Infinite God whose Being is forever transcendent—never concretely revealed as expressed in time. Only through communication can one manage to convey some of its limitless expanse of meaning.

How does one become conscious of communicative truth? Jaspers answers that it is only by thinking through all of the modes of the Encompassing; that "potential Existenz has the largest space in the world." [31] That is, Existenz should hold

---
[31] *Ibid.*, p. 98.

open before all of the world's actualities and possibilities, for it is only out of this that the will to communicate can work. Individual consciousness, however, is continually being restricted by that which one can directly communicate, but which, nevertheless, directly affects his existence. Then also, there are those who communicate with others whose Existenz is different from their own, yet who, through their own communication, affect their empirical existence and therein also their communication.

The will to communicate can be genuinely total only when the Encompassing is present in every form. But man cannot have Transcendence in time as a knowable absolute. What there is by way of an unconditioned truth can only be historical. It cannot be universally valid because it is practically impossible for any one man to hold fast to his own truth while recognizing the particularity of relative truths. But an open recognizing and acceptance of a plurality of truths can be equally as uninviting, and can lead to a total disruption in communication. Here Jaspers recognizes that there is not just Existenz, but Existenzen—a manifold of particular reference points which incur diverse goals and equally diverse modes of communication.

Only by men putting their struggles under rules, ceasing thereby to be concealed beasts, can there be developed the genuine strength of man which does not need to be satiated in power. Jaspers recognizes the dangers inherent in communication of a plurality of truths, all equally genuine, from the standpoint of empirical existence. In an optimistic tone he asserts that it is possible that a genuine communication might be accomplished through the recognition of potential existence on all sides so that an honest will-to-communication could be maintained on all sides. "A humanity might arise," he says, "which would not be weak, but capable of unforeseeable growth through openness, touched by every real Substance, a unique consciousness of limits to which the reality of action points, not to some dogmatically hardened, but rather to a genuine Transcendence." [32]

Even though there may seem to be not Existenz but Existenzen, a doctrine of an absolute plurality of truths is impossible. Each determinable standpoint absorbs the one who thinks it, closing the door against any real Transcendence, for the human condition is one which can be open only if it is to be fertile and productive and capable of growth. "To demand fulfillment and salvation in time, or even the picture of salvation, would be to conceal the problem of men who must always become themselves through communication." [33]

What must be avoided is any suggestion that the human situation can lead to a finished contentment. This would end it altogether. There is, accordingly, an unavoidable depth incurred by the unfulfillment of communication which only Transcendence can fill. There is something here which is akin to Marcel's ontological mystery. Transcendence is the universal bond which unites all in a demand which consumes existence. Neither Existenz nor Existenzen consume only partially revealed, one-sided, limited truths. Neither one can make anything clearly knowable; they can only for a moment touch the overwhelming impulses which, as resident in each person, are the actual power in genuine community.

The Truth is inaccessible. However, it is as though it could be recovered from its dispersion by communication. Or one could regard it as lying in the future, as something to go onwards in an unlimited disclosure. Above the world of an incessant, unlimited drive to communicate is the being of truth in Transcendence. This is not something to be achieved in the modes of the Encompassing, but only by surpassing these modes. The Truth of Transcendence is not something which

[32] *Ibid.*, p. 101.
[33] *Ibid.*, p. 103.

can be achieved by man in any one mode or in several of them. Truth in this case is something absolutely historical. "One can speak out of this experience, but not of it. The ultimate in thinking as in communication is silence." [34]

THE PRIORITY AND LIMITS OF RATIONAL THOUGHT

Although the modes of the Encompassing are structured, first as the Encompassing involving human existence which entails empirical existence, consciousness and spirit; and second as Being itself which in turn includes world and Transcendence, only the latter—Transcendence—has a priority in being. There is, furthermore, a hierarchy of Existenz over empirical existence, just as there is a hierarchy of spirit over consciousness in general. The whole idea of hierarchy, however, can never be taken as that of one level over another, but only on a single level.

There is another kind of priority, a formal one, which is true for thought. Jaspers points out that "The priority of thought means that no mode of the Encompassing can be present to us or become effective in us unless its content enters into the medium of thought." [35] The formal priority of thought then amounts to the fact that every mode of the Encompassing is turned into a possibility for human consciousness through the medium of thought. Also, it is the only medium through which the modes of the Encompassing can become related to one another.

There is a certain fatality, however, connected with the universality of thought in that thought can become itself self-destructive. That is, it is through thought that humanity not only apprehends itself but also chooses whether or not to ac-

---

[34] *Ibid.*, p. 106.
[35] *Ibid.*, p. 108.

cept thought in its widest possible dimensions or to restrict itself by its own self-binding power. When this fact of thought is recognized in its widest sense it becomes obvious that this is consciousness as such transcending itself. The impulse toward transcendence comes, however, not from the mere fact of consciousness but from the totality of all the modes of the Encompassing which man is.

The formal priority of thought is apparent through the fact of transcendence. That is, it is through the medium of thought that the nonrational becomes open to man. The nonrational can have meaning only in an indirect sense, only in the sense that it can be opposed to reason. "Thus," Jaspers writes, "I perceive ignorance itself through knowledge, and perfect ignorance only through the maximum of reason." [36] Accordingly, while the modes of the Encompassing achieve their fulfillment by use of concepts which reason provides, reason itself pushes on toward what is essentially unclear—to what is technically beyond itself. While the tools of reason are the concepts by which it attempts to reduce everything to something clearly thinkable, there is the nonobjective—the Encompassing itself which reason manages to reach through transcending. It is through this that active reason manages to go beyond the limits of empirical existence—beyond that which is outwardly demonstrable. For consciousness as such, objects of thought are directly intelligible as the presence of a concept which is identical for every understanding. Transcending thought, on the other hand, has an influence on man's inner life; it makes communicable that which has no apprehendable objective content. The result is that contradiction and paradox become meaningful in human existence. A rational a-logic thus arises, one which is a genuinely true reason in that it goes beyond the mere form of the understanding. But to keep transcending

---

[36] *Ibid.*, p. 110.

thought pure and clear one must avoid confusing its activity with that of consciousness as such. If its expression is taken in a direct literalness for the latter, the meaning of transcending thought will be perverted to the point where a false logic will arise—an untrue one in the form of the logic of the understanding. One fact which should be borne in mind is that, while transcending thought may appear to be impotent as for objectifying its transcending contents, it is itself a power which can be neither willed nor controlled by technique; a power which brings forth a revelation and transformation of interior man.

As a form of the rational a-logic, Jaspers refers to some of the concepts used by Kant in his deduction of the categories of thought. The categories of unity, plurality, substance et cetera were derived from a thinking consciousness (in this case Kant's own consciousness). But a thinking consciousness is itself governed by a transcendental unity of apperception which converts that which man encounters in the unity of an object. That is, a thing cannot *be* an object for man unless it is so unified that it can come under the direct apprehension of the thinking subject. This unity precedes the objectiveness of the thing in that it is a formally *a priori* condition. In other words, one can not conceive of the category of unity except by way of a transcendental apperception which is itself unified. The result, Jaspers points out, is that one arrives at formal logic either at a circle, where unity is explained through unity, or at a contradiction where unity is not unity.

The fact is, Jaspers says, that such circles and contradictions are real. Also, these are necessary in philosophy by the nature of things. He uses as an example the statement from Epimenides the Cretan who said, "All Cretans always lie when they speak." If this is true then Epimenides is also lying when he makes the statement. The content of what he says cancels the statement itself. What Jaspers wishes to make clear in this

92

regard is that there is a clear distinction between what can be ordinarily cognized as object and that which one can reach in philosophizing. This he says,

> is thought which, if it is to be touched upon, can permit nothing outside of its being thought, since it is the fundamental origin; it may be Being itself, or the condition of all objectivity as in the Kantian philosophy or it may be Existenz. We always have something which the understanding cannot grasp, but which is decisive for our certainty of being, which is less before us than present in our thought.[37]

The task of philosophy can now be seen in its unique aspect of having to bring its circles and contradictions to light rather than ruling them out as irrelevant or as irrational. While philosophy must certainly be prepared to handle what is empirically evident and to convert such entities into satisfactory concepts, it is nonetheless forced to accept the non-rational. Through consciousness, for example, one can apprehend empirical objects, and consciousness is itself an empirical fact. But the apparition of consciousness is not something which can be completely grasped or understood by consciousness itself. If it were, consciousness would be creative of itself —and this is the same mode of thought in which God is described as *causa sui*.

Existenz is also something which cannot be established as an empirical existent. But just as consciousness is the ground of one's knowledge of it, potential Existenz is the root of possibility for everything, and also the ground of Transcendence. Existence is also an example of the a-logical, for potential Existenz could properly belong to an act which has no apparent rationality to human consciousness, but which in itself would

---

[37] *Ibid.*, p. 115.

be perfectly clear. The truth of one's own communication, however, is decided by whether one can accept completely being alone before Transcendence. That is, one is completely a part of the Encompassing if one is ready to accept, but not to will, the possibility of one's own destruction. As Jaspers describes it, one becomes existentially "historical" only if one accepts his limited range of possibility. "Thus historicity is true," he says,

> only if, in its acceptance and thereby in the animation of one's own empirical existence, the greatest range of openness for Transcendence is secured. It is untrue—no longer itself but mere empirical existence, when its notion serves only to affirm the restrictions of empirical existence, a life which is precisely non-historical. In this way it would submerge empirical existence into itself in a fruitless anxiety over itself and its value.[38]

The meaning of Existenz can never be truly or adequately given through the use of the concepts of existential philosophy. The betrayal, however, does not lie in existential thought itself but in the way that the concepts are used to make certain assertions. The reason, Jaspers says, is that the truth of existentialist thought does not lie in its content as such, especially with reference to empirical existence, but in what happens to the person who thinks it. The falsity occurs when philosophic contents are used in order to gain some external end, "instead of producing by such concepts in oneself and in communication something which is man himself and not something meant by him. Such existential thought is either true, and then it is indissolubly connected with the being of the thinker; or it is a content to be known like any other, and then it is false." [39]

---

[38] *Ibid.*, p. 118.
[39] *Ibid.*, p. 121.

The problem of Existenz and human knowing poses an essential question concerning what can be deliberately planned as a legitimate human end, and what can not be. Another way of expressing the issue is to ask what can be desired and what disappears because one desires it. Jaspers uses as an example the idea of personality. If one deliberately contrives to achieve personality one achieves instead an "anxiously cultivated appearance." It is similarly the case for all substantial values. One can will "out of them" Jaspers says, but not actually will them.

The priority of thought needs now to be reexamined. When taken only in the sense of understanding it is entirely too narrow a meaning, for then thought exhausts itself in mechanical thinking, defining and ordering. Thought is essentially an encounter with Being inasmuch as one participates in it. The whole history of epistemology, or the knowledge of knowledge, from Aristotle to Kant has encountered two typical errors: one is the vacuity of a logic which has no direct connection with Being; the other is the fallacy of "absolute knowledge" of idealism which tries to convert the knowledge content in the modes of the Encompassing into a determinate knowledge of everything. In both cases, the element of thought which is conscripted bypasses the person, and in doing so it evades the meaning of the Encompassing. In the case of logic there is a philosophically indifferent knowledge of verbalism and mathematically graspable formalities—in other words, with the modalities of determinate knowledge. The error of idealism lies in its ambitious intention to convert everything, even the Godhead itself, into some intellectually apprehendable fact. Knowing, according to Jaspers, is the "self-consciousness of reason." "There is no truth," he says, "without some kind of communicability, and what is communicable always belongs on many levels to the various modes of the Encompassing in their interrelations, and always has its meanings within its sphere, not outside of it." [40]

A hope for a universal, unlimited, total knowledge is a false ideal. The truth of communicability is that which thinks out of Being itself in order, by thought, to advance back into Being. But while one can will Transcendence, there is always the danger of the understanding in its urge for something determinate, choosing some particular real thing for a transcendent historicity. This is man essentially willing himself to be particular rather than historical in his sense of being. To protect itself against this danger thought must hold itself open, free, in other words, for Transcendence; and again, according to Jaspers, "it must always reason in order to perceive that which is more than reason." [41]

---

[40] *Ibid.*, p. 121.
[41] *Ibid.*, p. 126.

CHAPTER IV

Chardin's "The Phenomenon of Man"

THE METHOD OF NATURALIST philosophers in the study of human nature has been to narrow the range of philosophical inquiry to a practical description of man's overt acts. The existentialists, on the other hand, have tried to examine man's overt acts in their widest sense of circumscription in order to come explicitly to terms with the form of *being* which is man. But there is another way of trying to make contact with the existential reality of mankind—making an exhaustive study of the human evolutionary story.

For Chardin, the method of arriving at a truly philosophical conception of man requires a profound understanding of the matter of the universe taken in its most minute form and comprehending it in its most subtle detail. In the early speculations of Democritus there was a suggestion that there are certain primary units into which all matter is ultimately divisible. That objects exist as particle collectives is evident even without the use of microscopes. But scientific research confirms the idea that structured compounds derive their unique sets of external properties from the differences in the infinitesimal particles of which each is composed. On the other hand, when one looks beyond the differences in the molecular structure of the compound particle to the composition of the sub-particle, there does appear to be a fundamental unity in all matter—a unity which is expressible in terms of energy components rather than in terms of mass.

While the concept of matter is necessary for understanding the story of the hominoid evolution, the full story of the production of a species can be written only by considering certain energy factors. Only by using terms which express matter's inner detail in its most originary context does the language of man's evolutionary history acquire its most precise meaning. No investigation of matter culminating in its being recognized as the substrate of consciousness can begin without taking account of its dynamic character. Its dynamic potential is one of its three faces; its capacity for multiplying combines by way of system the other two faces of totum and quantum. "The history of consciousness and its place in the world," Chardin wrote,

> remains incomprehensible to anyone who has not seen first of all that the cosmos in which man finds himself caught up constitutes, by reason of the unimpeachable wholeness of its whole, a *system*, a *totum* and a *quantum*, a system by its plurality, a totum by its unity, a quantum by its energy; all three within a boundless contour.[1]

The presence of "system" in the world should be obvious to anyone having even no more than a modicum of inductive power. It is a complex of inner organization which becomes apparent from its existential presence, and it is affirmed by consciousness in its inherent logical manner of assimilating and communicating what is impressed upon it. What one seeks, however, is not a clarification of the fact of system, but rather a clearer understanding of how the mesh of the universe op-

---

[1] Pierre Teilhard de Chardin, *The Phenomenon of Man* (New York: Harper & Brothers, 1959), p. 43.

erates as an ontological whole. But here one is already stepping past the boundary of naturalist inquiry. Ontological wholeness, even "ontology" itself, is not confirmed directly by empirical evidence, nor is it implied in any semantically correct proposition. On the other hand, the urge for the wholeness of evidence which is a demand for ontology is implicit in the existentialist impulse to see things in the widest range of the possible.

What becomes apparent upon close examination is that a system is no simple enlargement of a single totum. The whole planetary order, for example, does not consist of one system superimposed upon another. Chardin says that from the smallest dimension of matter in the vague circle of electrons to the vast interstellar space, there are heterogeneous envelopes, each composing matter in a different way. This is no repetition of a single theme on an increasing scale. There is the sense of an evolution of matter into more and more complex forms, and more and more intricate structures for each exchange. "The universal totum and quantum tend to express and define themselves in cosmogenesis." [2]

This evolution in matter can best be seen in its "gradual building up of the growing complexification of the various elements recognized in physical chemistry." [3] Beginning with the presence of luminous masses, not recognizable in terms of figure, there comes at some nodal point a swarming of corpuscular forms of matter. Thereafter there emerges on an atomic scale the harmonious series of elementary forms ranging from hydrogen to uranium. Atomic particles are the building blocks of an endless variety of compounds on an ascending scale of structural complexity leading to a certain critical stage at which there is the emergence of life. "This fundamental discovery," says Chardin, "that all bodies owe their origin

[2] *Ibid.*, p. 47.
[3] *Ibid.*, p. 47.

to arrangements of a single initial corpuscular type is the beacon that lights the history of the universe in their eyes. In its own way, matter has obeyed from the beginning that great law of biology to which we shall have to recur time and time again, the law of 'complexification.' " [4]

"Complexification," however, is the result of a synthesis which costs something in terms of energy. This involves an internal use of energy which is different from the use of energy in the tangential encounter of bodies. This difference in the use of energy is not something simply supposed on the basis of higher laws of biological organization. Modern physics has shown that at the extreme values reached by atomic movements there is a profound change realized in the mass of bodies; a change which strongly suggests a change in the direction of internal energy.

The fact of radioactive substance added to the fact of biological "complexification" makes it quite evident that the *within* of things can no longer be ignored. To understand the meaning of the *within* of things it is not required that one assumes tangential energy to perform in a way contrary to fact, but rather that one accepts the fact of energy being deployed in a different manner. For Chardin, tangential energy is that which links one element with all others of the same order—with those having the same complexity and the same centricity. Radial energy, on the other hand, is that which draws the particle toward a greater form of complexity.

For a certain degree of radial or "spiritual" energy there is produced a limited point of chemical bonding which permits of no further development. Such is the case of crystals. These are but mosaics of small elements such that the composite structure is incapable of further internal elaboration. But even as the world tends to crystallize, it does not do so completely.

---

[4] *Ibid.*, p. 48.

There are a far greater variety of unstable structures not so closed in on themselves. With the crystallization of mosaics of particles there occurred a release of new energy. Augmented by that which accrues from the atomic decomposition of radioactive substances, plus the continuing solar radiation, there appeared to be a surplus of energy which required some explanation of its fate. Chardin offers the hypothesis that this surplus of free energy when too weak to escape in incandescence was compensated by the power of reacting upon itself in the work of synthesis. As it does today, it passed into the formation of carbonates, hydrates, hydrites, and nitrates which are complexes of molecular structures. This is the work of polymerization. But where does polymerization occur, and how is it to be located with respect to the earth?

Chardin classifies the layers of the earth and its surroundings as having a five-area structure. The center of the earth consists in a metallic barysphere. Surrounding this inner core is a silicious lithosphere composed of rocks and minerals, which is itself surrounded by a hydrosphere of soil and water and pulverized rock. The surface of the earth is encompassed everywhere by an atmosphere consisting mainly of nitrogen, oxygen and carbon dioxide whose gaseous density is caused by the pull of gravity. Further out in space, where the pull is not as great, there is the stratosphere where these same gases are much less dense.

In Chardin's view the earth's surface and the atmosphere once composed a special envelope which was the temperate zone of polymerization. Ammonia, water and carbon dioxide were already floating in the rays of the sun, ready to take up the work of polymerization as a precondition from which the earliest instances of life could eventually spring. *"In this world,"* Chardin wrote, *"nothing could ever burst forth as final across the different thresholds successively transversed by evolution . . . which has not already existed in an obscure and primordial way.* If the organic had not existed on earth from the first moment at which it was possible, it would never have begun later." [5]

Because protein structures are the essential building blocks of life and because of the polymerization principle under which organic compounds emerge in series of intricate arrangements, it appears as if the gap between the living and the nonliving might be closed by an extension of the principle of radial energy. Polymerization occurs within limits not yet definable, and with every advance in complexity there is a corresponding increase in the capacity of the structure to relate itself still further to larger forms. It seems not only unnecessary but also futile to suppose that life requires some fecundating agent from the outer cosmos. To Chardin it seems to be much more probable that whatever fecundating agents were necessary were also present on this planet as a form of prelife and that life did emerge on the earth at the precise instant when it could occur, or it would not have occurred at all. There are two apparent facts which cause him to take this view. One is that of radial energy—the energy of synthesis under which particles undergo increasing "complexification." The second is that the chemical complexity of the earth increases in conformity with the law of thermodynamics. When these two facts are taken together, "they seem to tell us that prelife is no sooner enclosed in the nascent earth than it emerges from the torpor to which it appeared to have been condemned by its diffusion in space." [6]

THE ADVENT OF LIFE

That the cell is the essential unit of living structures is at once evident in any botanical or zoological direction one

[5] *Ibid.*, p. 73.
[6] *Ibid.*, p. 73.

may choose to look. It is the unit of granulation of living matter in much the same way that the atom is the granulated particle of the chemical world. Just as the atom is recognized as a primary assembly of mass points and energy particles, so is the cell the primary form in which living matter exercises a recognizable substance in that nitrogenous particles—albumin, fats, potassium and others—do not exist by themselves as primary units, but contribute to the function of that which is.

The main concern here is with the origin of the living cell and the transitional forms between large polymer molecules and the original cells. When one considers bacteria, viruses, enzymes, it is against a backdrop of higher plants and animals. This, Chardin says, "blinds our vision," for what one wants to see are the details of the *within* of things. Analysis of amorphous or polymorphous structures points back to the molecule. One is able to follow the same line of similarity among living units as is found among the nonliving—the same structural symmetry, the infinitesimal size. What separates one from the other is something which can be called proto-life—forms in which there are ingestion processes out of which more substantial structures emerge. On the other hand there is the world of the mega-molecule of astounding complexity leading up to the particles produced in ferments. But whatever links the one with the other, one can be certain, Chardin says, that the evolution of both types proceeded at an extremely slow pace.

Even though the enveloping condition which induced the succession of structures leading toward the original apparition of the cell may be now lost from sight, there is much that is present and discoverable which indicates the existence of the transitional forms postulated by the theory of evolution. For example, the gaping void which was once supposed to exist between protoplasm and mineral matter is being filled through the discovery of certain molecular aggregates of incredible size and complexity. Moreover, the presence of both animate and inanimate substances obliges one to recognize that their differences in structure involve also differences in duration; that these have sprung into being and were dispersed in space at different time points. "As a naturalist," Chardin says, "I am obliged to recognize that the assumption of a dimensional *milieu* in which space and time are organically combined is the only way we have found to explain the distribution around us of animate and inanimate substances." [7] This space-time milieu becomes applicable even in the study of animate substances alone. For while naturalists have been unable to give a scientific explanation for Linnaeus' classification of animals into a structure of order, families, genera, et cetera, "We know that the system of Linnaeus merely represents a present-day cross section of a genealogical *tree* whose principal branches were the phyla coming down through the centuries." [8]

Why the millions of years separating the advent of life from the time when the planet cooled and the waters and rocks began to separate? Considering the astounding complexity of living structures today, especially that of man, this is not at all surprising. No profound change, Chardin says, could ever occur except through long periods of the maturing of the preconditions. The emergence of the mega-molecules must have been narrowly dependent on the chemical and thermal conditions prevailing on the planet. Then also, once the transformation began it must have been extended to a sufficiently large mass of matter to form an envelope large enough to have been the basis for life when it too could spread.

The unique position of the cell becomes starkly evident when it is recognized that viscosity, osmosis and catalysis—

---

7 *Ibid.*, p. 83.
8 *Ibid.*, p. 83.

characteristic activities of molecular structures—are here brought under the dominance of a nucleus. Selfhood at last emerges with a recognizable center. "Indefinite as are the possible modulations of the fundamental theme, inexhaustible as are the various forms it assumes in nature, the cell remains in all cases essentially true to itself." [9] The atom, the crystalline, the polymer are all surpassed by a new structure whose radial energy far exceeds that of any other. For one thing, the cell is equipped to enter the flux of being and to add to the immense diversity in which simple matter can become compounded. After undergoing its genesis by way of an external revolution, it next proceeds by way of an intrinsic one. "If we have already endowed the long chain of atoms, then molecules, then mega-molecules, with the obscure and remote sources of rudimentary free activity," says Chardin, "it is not by a totally new beginning but by a *metamorphosis* that the cellular revolution should express itself psychically." [10]

A new kind of activity is now expressed: one which is not necessarily dependent on external chemical and thermal conditions. By metamorphosis a substance changes, evolves from within, under the influence of its inner radial energy. Also, because the cell is a system of energy exchange with its environment, there is now a determinate relation established between the *within* and the *without*. The determination of a *within* of things can be demonstrated by a closed figure suddenly having a center, or by a circle augmenting its order of symmetry by tracing out a sphere. But here, by a new mode of arrangement between the *within* and the *without* there is acquired a new level of synthesis. "The increase of the synthetic state of matter involves . . . an increase of consciousness for the milieu synthesized." [11] Although it is not yet known

9 *Ibid.*, p. 87.
10 *Ibid.*, p. 88.
11 *Ibid.*, p. 89.

what enters at what critical moment, there is no doubt that there does occur a change in the nature of a particle. Chardin uses the phrase "change in the nature of the state of consciousness of the particle," apparently taking consciousness in a somewhat broad, undifferentiated sense to mean a forward leap in spontaneity.

Chardin's speculations have brought empirical evidence to support the position that the life impulse originated through a long, sustained process in which the internal complexity of molecular structures was gradually increased. From what can be known of living structures, life requires a superorganization of matter, of internal elaboration far in excess of that of the nonliving. From the internal side of mega-molecules pushing themselves forward in an exploration of new modes of synthesis, a sudden explosion of internal energy boosts structures already synthesized into new modes of affinity. "Such an external realization," he says,

> of an essentially new type of corpuscular grouping, allowing the more supple and better centered organization of an unlimited number of substances at all degrees of particulate magnitude, involves a double and radical metamorphosis (in regard to what is specifically original in it) in terms of which we can reasonably define the critical passage from the molecule to the cell—the transit to life.[12]

One inference which researchers seem to make is that life now originates only from life. The period for the transformation from nonliving to living matter is over. The elements involved in the apparition of the cell have become lost in sediments transformed long ago. There is, Chardin suggests, a law running through history which is the "automatic suppression

---

[12] *Ibid.*, p. 89.

of evolutionary peduncles." The breaking out of a new phylia or strain is accompanied by a hardening of the ways of life assigned to each one so that these do not metamorphosize into forms of life radically different from their own, but retain their basic structural characteristics. Even though the conditions which caused life to spring from the nonliving are not present and observable, there are, Chardin insists, other ways by which one can read reality. To try to envisage the beginning of life amid the material superstructure which now exists would be to start at the wrong point. One must instead try to imagine the world as it was likely to be at the prelife period—a world enveloped by a total ocean with but a few signs of continents beginning to protrude through the surface of the water. The water was then doubtless warmer and fraught with some of the free valences which have since become stabilized. It is possible to imagine early particles of protoplasm with or without nuclei. The smallness of bacteria—one five thousandths of a millimeter—and their staggering number present a world teeming with ultramicroscopic bits of protoplasm about to harden into substantial centers of selfhood which, by way of sudden bursts of radial energy, managed to secure larger forms of livelihood for themselves.

Several things seem to have been both highly probable and necessary. One is that the passage from mega-molecule to cells occurred at a single isolated point in place and time. A second is that there were numerous strands leading from one to the other which led to the possibility of cellular diversification and higher syntheses occurring in a variety of forms. Then there is a third—more significant perhaps than either of the others—which is that individual cells were equipped with a special capacity for symbiosis, or life in common. Clustered groups were no mere aggregates having their own routines of existence. The symbiosis involved a unity under a new structural bond—a multilayered bond ranging from the internal cohesion of polymer elements to the new appendages which would augment the life within whose potential the lower elements had become locked.

Despite the possibility that this transition occurred in a wide variety of ways, what seems to be positive evidence of the presence of a single life principle is the remarkable similarity of cellular composition and structure. "Biologists have noticed that, according to the chemical group to which they belong, the molecules incorporated into living matter are all asymmetrical in the same way, that is to say if a pencil of polarized light is passed through them they all turn the plane of the beam *in the same direction*—either they are all right-rotating or all left-rotating according to the group taken." [13] But what is even more remarkable, Chardin says, is that all living things contain exactly the same types of enzymes and vitamins. So amid the diversification of species, the life principle is astoundingly uniform and precise. Moreover, this uniformity of the conditions of existence extends even further than to the *within*. The cosmic conditions which once supported the original leap are now transformed into those which form a protective envelope which sustains life in the myriads of forms in which it is now expressed.

THE EXPANSION OF LIFE

Having now constructed a hypothesis of the way the earliest particles in which the life impulse was believed to abound combined among themselves to engender new and novel forms of structural unity, Chardin turns to an investigation of the processes by which internal articulation might take place.

As there are now one-celled structures which have hardened into lasting forms of specialization, there were also

---

[13] *Ibid.*, p. 95.

those in the early age of life which persisted in a simple structural unity. There were also simple collections—aggregates of clusters of cells which existed in the barest sense of a collective unity. Then there were those more advanced forms of life in which strong central foci of being became generated in such a way that the tiny cellular components did not themselves endeavor toward independent existence, but rather became subordinate to a superior type of genetic incorporation. Chardin designates this special kind of evolutionary phenomenon as *orthogenesis*. This is no mere spreading out of an increasing variety of life particles. "We get diversification, the growing specialization of factors forming a single genealogical sequence —in other words, the apparition of the *line* as a natural unity distinct from the *individual*." [14]

Orthogenesis contains the deeper meanings of cosmic intent than are revealed in the determinate structures of molecules and the free play of chance. Cell division seems to occur because of the inability of the single one to maintain itself in a single expanding form. Because the surface areas of bodies tending to be spherical vary as the squares of the radii while the volumes of the respective bodies vary as the cubes of the internal radii, cells reach that critical point where they are no longer able to support their inner growth activities through surface osmosis. Their splitting up is a way of preserving life in the face of an inherent fragility. But this bifurcation is but one side of the total process. Always within it there is the counter tendency toward agglutination, toward the formation of new centers of being and a surge toward more articulate forms of totality. What is becoming apparent is that evolution moves toward securing a higher form of consolidation. Out of an original move toward new forms of collective unity, new structures, clearly differentiable from each other, break forth as phylia.

---

[14] *Ibid.*, p. 108.

The concept of *phylum* is indispensable for an understanding of the tree of life. It is, first of all, a collection of cells more advanced in the metazoic stage than simple aggregates, and it has a centrality belonging to itself alone. By utilizing mega-molecules, it is capable of ramifying, of utilizing new determinate structures of the larger molecules by its inherent process of probing for new extremities which involve it in a more complete mode of interaction with its environment. It attains full maturity when it has achieved the utmost in consolidating and individuating all the extremities of its various ramifications.

There has not been one, but many, phyla evolving through centuries of evolution, growth and exploration. What appears to be a solid fact of nature is that the whole earth pulsates with life pushing itself forward in a variety of primordial life-bearing forms. In its preliminary manifestations, life remains mysterious because the original peduncles in which it was established are now lost from sight. But the evidence of the biological achievement is undeniably present in the various biota which impress themselves, and also their differences, upon one's intellectual vision. Numerous separate phyla have budded at various points and have gone on to form separate verticils which, in turn, are the main stalks which leaf out in whatever ways the life of the being can be solidified. In every case there is a surge toward a greater measure of spontaneity; and this is not, Chardin explains, just an interlocking succession of structural types, but the phenomenon of an inner sap rising and spreading out of consolidated existents. "Right at the base," he says, "the living world is constituted by consciousness clothed in flesh and bone. From the biosphere to the species is nothing but an immense ramification of psychism seeking for itself by means of different forms." [15]

---

[15] *Ibid.*, p. 151.

The psychic impulse is the strongest, most durable of all.[16] There appears to be a definite link between this and the degree of adaptability and spontaneity which living structures possess, and correspondingly, with the hold which they have on their existence. The most evident tendency of the psychic impulse is to escape being frozen in any kind of limited behavior. The case of insects is a classic example. An insect cannot grow beyond a particular size without becoming dangerously fragile. It can never possess a brain large enough for any massive breakthrough of consciousness. What has happened, Chardin says, is that it became extroverted and therefore frozen in certain necessary reflexes. The price for sustaining life on this level was the disappearance of individual particularization absorbed by function. Where there is practically no pronounced psychic spontaneity, there is little room for self-expression as an individual.

At the other extreme of biological size there is an example of the dinosaur whose tiny brain was no more than a string of lobes, smaller in thickness than a human's spinal cord. Here was a verticil which had developed a large body. It was equipped with strong legs and endowed with herbivorous habits, and it fulfilled its maximum of biological efficiency without any appreciable spurt in consciousness. Only among the mammals, and especially among the primates, did the tendency toward hominization continue to push forward, driven, perhaps, by an inner impulse toward psychic performance. What is here regarded as psychic is, however, something other than the thinking or acting of a subject. The overt acts of phyla—testing, exploring, and making use of openings for

---

[16] Because of the long period in evolutionary time through which the psychic impulse had to travel before becoming openly expressed in consciousness, the psychic impulse had to be the most durable of all. It had to wait for its apparition as consciousness until all the requisite conditions for its emergence were present.

novel performance—acts which are characteristic of man's reflective consciousness—are manifest in a psychic groping toward the production of the physical requirements for conscious behavior. At each step, however, there is also present that incipient tendency toward the hardening of selfhood into permanent strains which follows a specific set of functions in response to a physical environment, each with its own set of reflexes or automata. Animal consciousness is an example of animal psychism achieving the level of ego awareness and awareness of an environment, even though animal response to its natural environment is governed largely by instinctive reflexes. Animals know, but they do not know that they know, and they are not equipped to engage themselves in a reflective analysis about the physical milieu in which they exist. Animals certainly communicate, but they have never constructed a set of symbols to contain and to enlarge what can be known by them. Accordingly, there is no animal culture, no animal history except in terms of biological evolution, and no animal civilization.

Morphologically, the difference between animal and man is slight. What differences there are can be expressed statistically in terms of cranial capacity, facial contours, and other physical features. But the reflexive apparatus in man is a kind of superiority which far exceeds any kind of psychic behavior in animals. The facts of evolution in terms of change of structure and function are apparent in biological science. But what science has so far failed to acknowledge is the persistence of certain grades of the life impulse which point toward hominization. That the entire earth literally pulsates with life is evident in the great variety of different phyla. But, Chardin insists, there is amid this variety a *main line* embodying in a modified form all the appurtenances of the others and containing the superior modes of adaptability and socialization culminating in consciousness.

REFLECTION

What has been described as consciousness is, in a singular sense, the awareness—the cognition of the facts of one's own here and now existence. But when one speaks of the rise of consciousness it is not in this context. It is instead the involvement of a fulfilling plan toward an articulate type of existence. In the case of man, this culminated in the psychic process of doubling back to produce an organ by which consciousness would break forth to involve itself transitively in the world. In this case it did not become canalized into frozen routines of automatic behavior. The psychic composition of this new congealment contained an inner spontaneity which made the act of reflection possible. The freeing of psychic activity from having to follow the laws of molecular behavior allowed it to enter into a new and more volatile field of action, that of logic—of the rules or laws of reflection itself. Life, being an organ of consciousness, could not continue to advance without transforming itself in depth. It had, like all growing magnitudes in the world, to become different to remain itself.[17]

The emergence of consciousness as self-awareness is a phenomenon of deeper meaning than that of a psychic impulse exerting evolutionary pressures in the metamorphosis of phyla. The transit to reflection involved a change of state. But this was not all. There was also the beginning of another kind of life which cannot be explained by physiological processes as they are understood. Reflective processes have to be understood in terms of their own activity. Chardin says:

---

[17] Chardin says: "The point here is that this 'something'—construction of matter or construction of beauty, systems of thought or systems of action—ends up always by translating itself into an augmentation of consciousness and consciousness in its turn, as we know, is nothing less than the substance and heart of life in the process of evolution." *Ibid.*, p. 178.

Where intelligence is concerned, "to be posited" does not mean "to be achieved." As soon as the child is born, it must breathe or it will die. Similarly the reflective psyche centre, once turned in upon itself, can only subsist by means of a double movement which is in reality one and the same. It centres itself further on itself by penetration into a new space, and at the same time it centres the rest of the world around itself by the establishment of an ever more coherent and better organized perspective in the realities which surround it. We are not dealing with an immutably fixed focus but with a vortex which grows deeper as it sucks up the fluid at the heart of which it was born. The ego only persists by becoming ever more itself, in the measure in which it makes everything else itself. *So man becomes a person in and through personification.*[18]

To what end do these inner reflective processes lead? These were not, it seems, just more refined ways of dealing with the requirements of the animal world. The influence of radial energy was not only to augment the ways of physiological satisfaction. For it was the process of internal reflection which led to the emergence of man as a hominoid species when hominization constituted a new dimension in existence. It constituted, for one thing, an instantaneous leap from instinct to thought. But when the threshold of thought is reached, life has not only reached the rung on which man now stands, it has also begun to overflow the boundaries which confined it by the exigencies of physiology. That is, hominization consists in the production of a species which is not just determinate in terms of physiological requirements, but more specifically by the phyletic spiritualization of the forces contained in the animal world.

Where, and in exactly what way, man as a thinking being came upon the scene cannot be known. "Between the last

---

[18] *Ibid.*, p. 172.

strata of the Pliocene age, in which man is absent, and the next, in which the geologist is dumbfounded to find the first chipped flints, what has happened? And what is the true meaning of this leap?" [19] One thing seems to be certain; man did not come alone as one single, silent individual. When one examines the indestructible stone implements which primordial man fashioned, it is quite evident that he existed all over the old world. One can estimate that man began to appear in the early part of the Quaternary era. The *Pithecanthropus* of Java and the *Sinanthropicus* of China are definitely hominoidal in their anatomy even though they are sometimes classified as prehumanoidal when compared with modern man's intellectual capacity.

The change in evidence from the Quaternary era to the Neolithic period reveals a striking increase in psychic influence. Although the Neolithic period is sometimes treated with disdain by historians for its lack of definite, written evidence, there are many pieces of evidence which subtly suggest the existence of a civilizing activity. Tools were becoming much more refined; pottery and polished stones were making their appearance. Man was also beginning to make use of parcels of land for cultivation rather than following the line of the nomad and the hunter. But even more striking was the change in man's relation to his fellowmen. On the one hand, hominization led to a dispersal of the members of the species when it split up into separate, egocentered centers of life, each pursuing its own selected goals of achievement. On the other hand, there was a countermovement toward unification. The solid facts of human existence, Chardin insists, do not support the position that psychogenesis invariably points toward a continual diffusion at this, its upper level. Just as when lower phyla interpenetrate each other mutually to combine their

---

[19] *Ibid.*, p. 164.

radial energy in bundles, so is this similarly the case for man. What, Chardin asks, would have become of humanity if it had been left to spread indefinitely through its internal affinities alone? For centuries, from the Neolithic age forwards, no serious obstacle checked the spread of human waves over the surface of the globe, and this may have accounted for the slowness of their social evolution. But in later ages, having to fit more tightly together, these waves began to recoil upon themselves so that human elements began to interpenetrate each other more and more. The internal pressure of the closer human community incurred a sudden rapid increase in intellectual growth and technological specialization. "Under conditions of distribution," Chardin says,

> which in any other initial phylum would have led long ago to the break up into different species, the human verticil as it spreads out remains entire, like a gigantic leaf whose veins, however distinct, remain always joined in a common tissue. With man we find indefinite interfecundation on every level, the blending of genes, anastomoses of races in civilizations or political bodies.[20]

From *geogenesis* to *biogenesis* to *psychogenesis* there is now added another dimension to the pulsating world process —*noogenesis*. *Noogenesis* is the process of thought turning inwards upon itself as well as outward to construct a lasting framework and a depository of its own achievement. This is the point of release from the psychological boundaries within which man existed for so many thousands of years. Phyletic spiritualization can be regarded as a rebellion against the meaninglessness of inanimate existence. In *noogenesis* one encounters something of a second rebellion, a revolt against the closeness in which individualized existence, when predomi-

---

[20] *Ibid.*, p. 124.

nantly vegetative, found itself. Here was a new outburst of phyletic spiritualization, one which led to a form of centrality which was radically different from that of biological individuality. This was a phyletic venture which took place entirely on the advanced level of human consciousness: one which spawned the rise of art and symbol in an ever widening expanse of human *culture*. In human culture the inner radial energy involved in man's evolutionary growth took an entirely new turn as the pressure toward biological "complexification" dropped off. Phyletic ingenuity—that which had always given rise to evolutionary novelty and innovation—was now expressing itself in the production of new expression forms of consciousness rather than as forms of biological advance.

What has been a persistent problem for men has been learning how to assess this ever-growing achievement. "For many of our contemporaries," Chardin writes,

> mankind still remains something unreal unless materialized in an absurd way. For some it is an abstract entity, or even a mere conventional expression; for others it became a closely-knit organic group in which the social element can be transcribed literally in terms of anatomy and physiology. It appears either as a general idea, a legal entity, or else as a gigantic animal.[21]

In any case one fails to assess the whole correctly. Would it not be necessary to introduce a concept of the superindividual, not as some enlarged image of the ordinary man, but a concept which is an adequate configuration of mankind—of man in the sense of his plurality? All stages up through hominization have been a coalescence of elements, and in psychogenesis this same coalescence shapes the confluence of psychic factors in the accumulation of the *noogenesis*. But the

---

[21] *Ibid.*, p. 246.

nature of mankind insofar as it can be thought of as pointing to something beyond the mere fact of a collective has often been veiled in illusion. The convergent effect of the *noogenesis* upon mankind needs some clarification.

Chardin describes knowledge as the "twin sister of mankind." That is, mankind and knowledge grew up together. The measure of man's ripening into fulfillment has been the measure of his knowledgeable command of his environment. But man and his ways of knowing have been cast in a religious evolution, and both have fallen into the same disrepute. However, the solution seems to be neither abrogating mankind nor repudiating knowledge. "Nowadays thanks to a philosophy which has given a meaning and a consecration to our thirst to think all things, we can glimpse that unconsciousness is a sort of ontological inferiority or evil, since the world can fulfill itself in so far as it expresses itself in a systematic and reflective perception." [22] Knowledge for its own sake may appear as an ideal good, but more specifically what is ideal in knowledge is increased action for increased being.

Unanimity, as a form of convergent consciousness, is open to a variety of interpretations and applications. Natural egoism tends to make one regard a central focus of being as something contrary to the idea of free individuality. But the fact of consciousness and communicability, seen in the light of metasynthesis accounting for the advanced stages of phyletic development, cannot but impress one with the concept of a whole plurality of interdependent creatures combining their energies in a mutual reinforcement toward an act of single conscious reflection. In simple language, sociality is founded upon the fact of *agreement,* if not in each deed or act, at least in the principle of the act. Without reflective unanimity society would not be possible at all, because, in this case, com-

_____
[22] *Ibid.*, p. 248.

munication simply could not occur. What should be altogether obvious is that no one individual can advance intellectually except by the interpenetration of his thinking with the thinking of others. Turning away from the possibility of reflective unanimity and its inherent requirements leads only to an involvement in other ways of collective synthesis; for individuals are equipped in many ways to reduce large multitudes to order, mass movements scientifically assembled.

The Million in rank and file on the parade ground, the Million standardized in the factory; the Million motorized—and all this only ending up with Communism and National Socialism and the most ghastly fetters. So we get the crystal instead of the cell; the ant-hill instead of brotherhood. Instead of the upsurge of consciousness which we expected, it is mechanization that seems to emerge inevitably from totalization.[23]

What is the alternative to this way of materializing the human collective? Is it possible that consciousness has not yet advanced to the point where it can more sufficiently detach itself from the touch of the psychological? What stands in the way of postulating a hyperconsciousness? Instead of a fear of a more subtle, yet the same kind of, enslavement, could not the possibility of a hyperconsciousness suggest a new freedom?

There is the obvious fact of unanimity as it has already been expressed. Human society has become possible only because of the remarkable convergence of its value goals and its susceptibility to a logic of order. Far from having to vacillate between setting up an independent *I* which is set up at the antipodes of the *All,* and the other extreme, which is the diminishing of the ego in its absorption in a collective, this interdependence leads necessarily to neither, but to a further

---

23 *Ibid.,* p. 156.

119

evolutionary ascent of consciousness. What has been admitted by most materialists, and even gnostics, is that *evolution is an ascent toward consciousness,* and also that the process undergoes a series of involutions or acts of recoil upon itself. But could the curve of hominization lead to differences rather than culminate in some supreme consciousness? Chardin says that this would be manifestly in error. "It is only by hyperreflection—that thought can extrapolate itself. Otherwise how could it garner our conquests which are all made in the field of what is reflected?" [24]

If it is difficult for one to imagine the fact of universal consciousness converging toward a point which is not at the level of the personal, but the hyperpersonal, it is because the approach to this matter is from the wrong perspective. Any attempt to imagine this in terms of egoistic experience alone can only fail because the fact of egoism necessarily involves an awareness center which is closed in on itself. The same basic differences between the All and the one would continue to govern one's personal perspective. Accordingly, it is not oneself but the noosphere itself which needs to be held as the object of inquiry. "All our difficulties," Chardin writes,

> and repulsions as regards the opposition between the All and the person would be dissipated if only we understood that, by structure, the noosphere (and more generally the world) represents a whole that is not only closed but also *centered.* Because it contains and engenders consciousness, space-time is necessarily of a *convergent nature.* Accordingly its enormous layers, followed in the right direction, must somewhere ahead become involuted to a point which we might call *Omega,* which fuses and consumes them integrally in itself.[25]

_____
[24] *Ibid.,* p. 258.
[25] *Ibid.,* p. 259.

There is one thing one must recognize about consciousness when used in the sense of phyletic spiritualization, and this is that the latter is only partially revealed in human consciousness. Human consciousness is one of the many nodal points at which phyletic spiritualization becomes manifest; the most significant, perhaps, from the point of view of the entire cosmos, but nevertheless limited and one-sided. For human consciousness is never capable of effecting the transformation of the materials of the earth into that kind of structured matter which produces life or which sustains it. In bits and fragments it contributes to the noosphere, but even in this contribution it does not truly understand what it is doing. It only obeys its impulses to think and to construct; impulses which are rooted in the psyche.

What moves man toward a fulfillment of the noosphere is not just the coldly analytic force of reason alone, but also his capacity for love. Here is a term so intimately subjective that psychologists, who are required to accept it as a datum of human behavior, tend to reduce it to some biological drive, while scientists disregard it and philosophers hesitate to deal with it at all. But the love impulse is far too universal to be explained as biological, or even as psychological, passion. As a general property of all life, love is the general tendency to unite; a tendency which is easily recognized in many different modalities in animal behavior. Further down among the more rudimentary forms of the life world the love impulse is almost imperceptible. But however faint its appearance, the love impulse is a property of the within of things. Chardin says, "if there were no internal propensity to unite, even at the prodigiously rudimentary level—indeed in the molecule itself—it would be physically impossible for love to appear higher up, with us, in 'hominized' form." [26]

[26] *Ibid.*, p. 264.

Human love is an impulse, an unconscious drive, which is neither understood nor controllable. But it does not require very deep reflection to recognize that love is also energy; the energy causing the involution of individual consciousness upon itself, uniting all, binding all into a total body of consciousness on earth. Just as the energy in phyletic spiritualization spreads life over the whole earth so also does the energy of love exert its sense of infinity throughout the whole universal consciousness of man. Universal love, the love for all mankind, becomes incarnate in the person of Christ. "If the world is convergent," Chardin wrote,

> and if Christ occupies its centre, then the Christogenesis of St. Paul and St. Peter is nothing else and nothing less than the extension, both awaited and unhoped for, of that noogenesis in which cosmogenesis—as regards our experience—culminates. Christ invests himself organically with the very majesty of his creation. And it is in no way metaphorical to say that man finds himself capable of experiencing and discovering his God in the whole length, breadth and depth of the world in movement.[27]

One may not assume that the appearance of Christ on earth was for the purpose of cutting short the natural curve of hominization. True, He did offer eternal salvation to the faithful, but this salvation is not to be construed as a remaking of the earth. It was the promise of a blessed condition after death that the soul would rest in perfect union with God in pure love and sublimity. But the essence of Christianity on earth has quite another meaning and purpose. By becoming immersed in things material, Christ, the man, invested himself organically in the world and assumed the control and the leadership of man's spiritual evolution.

---

[27] *Ibid.*, p. 297.

Christ, principle of universal vitality because sprung up as man among men, put himself in the position (maintained ever since) to subdue under himself, to purify, to direct and superanimate the general ascent of consciousness into which he inserted himself. By a perennial act of communion and sublimation, he aggregates to himself the total psychism of the earth.[28]

What is the rest of the story of mankind on earth? The idea of a collective is somehow inevitable, for psychogenesis points inexorably toward greater and greater unanimity. But every form of collectivization deliberately contrived by man tends in some way to destroy him, or at least to reduce the quality of his being by reducing his function. Chardin quite emphatically recognizes that the Omega point of human consciousness will never be realized in that way. Nevertheless, whatever evolutionary pressures can be detected today are noticeable in terms of their effect toward a reflective control over the environment. The same three psychobiological properties, the power of invention, the capacity for attraction (or repulsion) and the demand for irreversibility, which once produced the original step toward reflection, continue to be felt or sensed in the drive toward increased socialization. The fact of human freedom, however, makes it possible for a setback to occur in the movement toward a collective threshold of reflection. Hence Chardin feels compelled to recognize that there are several questions which the philosopher must in some way handle. One concerns what place remains for man's freedom in a supposed continuing ascent of consciousness. A second question raised the point about the value assigned to spirit as opposed to that accorded to matter. A third concerns what distinctions are to be had between God and the World in the way of regarding the theory of cosmic involution.

---

[28] *Ibid.*, p. 294.

Any answer which one might try to give for the first question would have to be provisional; an Omega point of convergence of the curve of hominization is by no means certain. It is true that there are "noogenic" forces of compression, organization and interiorization which have not relaxed their pressures upon mankind. But one must not forget, Chardin says, that there would have to be arrangements of greater complexities which, in turn, would not operate except by the two related methods of a groping utilization of favorable cases and reflective invention. A historical survey of man's progress in the past is a fairly easy task when compared with that of projecting this progress in the future. It is quite difficult to engage in predictability when one is faced with two factors—chance at the bottom of a possible occurrence and freedom at the top.

With regard to the second question, Chardin says that matter and spirit do not present themselves as things or as "natures" but rather as related "variables," and the concern is not some secret essence of each, but the curve in function of space and time. At this level of reflection, "consciousness" is not some subsistent entity in itself, but an "effect" of complexity. Once this definition of consciousness is assumed, nothing stops one, he says, "from prolonging downward toward the lower complexities under an invisible form the spectrum of the 'within'." [29] On the other hand, the same psychic element which shows itself as subtending the totality of the entire phenomenon shows also a growing tendency toward mastery and autonomy. At first, it is the focus of each individual element which by its own arrangement engenders and controls its related focus of consciousness. But later this equilibrium is reversed so that at the threshold of reflection the higher focus of consciousness itself takes charge. Still later this sec-

---

[29] *Ibid.*, p. 307.

ond focus of consciousness breaks away from its temporal-spatial frame to become a part of the supreme focus Omega. "In the perspectives of cosmic involution, not only does consciousness become co-extensive with the universe, but the universe rests in equilibrium and consistency, in the form of thought, on a supreme pole of interiorization." [30] Finally, with respect to the third question of the relation between God and the World, Chardin says that the idea of a converging universe presupposes a preexisting and transcendent center of unification. This is a suggestion of pantheism, but not necessarily of God's being literally present in nature. It is a pantheism, but only insofar as the reflective centers of the world are "one with God." Evolution requires the concept of convergence, for in no way could species begin to ripen into existence. The presence of a collective and stabilizing function is always required for the definition of this concept. But this, Chardin insists, "is obtained not by identification (God becoming all) but by the differentiating and communicating action of love (*God all in everything*). And this is essentially orthodox and Christian." [31]

---

[30] *Ibid.*, p. 308.
[31] *Ibid.*, p. 308.

CHAPTER V

The Common Philosophy

THE TASK OF PHILOSOPHY among the cosmologists in Ionia was to discover a fundamental element, some primary mode of *being*, which was the existential ground of all things. These men did not express their ideas in a sophisticated terminology; in fact the language of Thales, Anaximenes, Anaximander, Heraclitus and Anaxagoras was quite ordinary, and their thinking seemed to gravitate toward that which was involved in daily experience. That these men came to regard the ultimate substratum of all things to be something material is what one would expect. But while they did use simple figures of speech, their thinking aroused a number of metaphysical ideas which endured and became essential to future philosophical constructions. Thales's figurative use of "water" could well have meant some homogeneous medium out of which diverse *being* flows, and the "Universal flux" of which Heraclitus wrote could stand for universal light energy which consumes as well as arouses things into existence. Certainly that which receives everything into itself could be also that encompassing medium from which all things emerge. Then too, there was the sun—in its fiery splendor—which perhaps engendered the idea of an all-embracing force which holds things in a united whole. Imagining the sun as Apollo driving his chariot each day across the sky was no doubt a pleasing bit of fiction. But the Greek scholar knew that such notions belong only to the worlds of myth and fantasy. Greek intelligence understood the use of metaphor, but it also understood the need of explanation. It was not long after philosophy began that the Greek thinkers began extrapolating causes for effects whose connections with tangible realities had been obscure. The designation of something as an ordering element had been done as a matter of intellectual convenience. But one question continued to present itself: Was not an ordering element itself ordered? Water, air, fire, and even earth might each be that instrument by which matter assumes form and dimension. But now it would be required to show how these, in turn, had been caused to be. In the works of Anaxagoras and Heraclitus, the idea of a universal *mind* was beginning to emerge. It was not enough merely to think of things being in some way *ordered*: It was the apparition of order in the world of appearances which readied these appearances for man's abstractive intelligence. But the apparition of order itself was arousing human consciousness and its attendant curiosity to the point where it could not be ignored or put down.

Primordial philosophy sprang out of man's wonder and his power to be amazed. One can readily understand how the earliest forms of philosophical speculation came about through the outward thrust of curiosity. As a universal science, however, philosophy includes within its own purview curiosity itself—or more directly—that which is curious; and to understand this, Jung's "projective" idea is needed. The myths which sprang up in connection with early Greek cosmology and those which colored Greek drama must be understood as a means for satisfying a deep-rooted craving of the psyche—a craving for self-identification. It is not at all surprising that the object of man's philosophical wonder should come full round to a study of man himself. Also, it is not surprising that several schools, the Heraclitian, the Eleatic, and the Pythagorean, recognized that man was himself a part of the entire order of *being*. They were also beginning to venture toward the idea that man's own intelligence was a canalization of universal order itself.

This canalization of universal order in man's intelligence did not suggest, however, that man was circumscribed in the phenomenal world by an iron ring of cause and effect. Actually, cause-effect ideas were only loosely apparent in early Greek speculation, for there were still some lingering traces of the older mythology which had shaped Greek thinking for many centuries before. One of the main characteristics of mythology was its nonliteral joining of fantasy with fact. But while the idea of metaphysical free will had not ripened in any philosophical system, man's designated place in the natural order and his participation in natural laws was supplemented by a certain personal freedom to flout or to evade such laws. A growing consciousness of man's fallibility was becoming apparent in the ethics of the Orphics, the Pythagoreans, and others. In the great works of Plato and Aristotle, ethics assumes a central position in an ever-growing ontology. In the works of Plato especially, where Socrates is the main ethical figure, there is a fruition of what had been given mainly in conjecture in earlier works. By use of myth and symbol, the order which is given from without is also made to convey fragmented bits of the perceptual self. The idea that *order* is primarily a conceptual experience rather than just an empirical arrangement of material things also began to make its impress on human consciousness. That is, man's acknowledgement of order was an affirmation that his own reflective subjectivity could unite him with his world of outer experience in the conceptual process. Man's earliest participation in creative knowing came about when he began to impose his own subjective design upon that which was given from without. In this way the *without* was the intelligible reference—that which needed to be and could be understood. It took but one more step for man to include himself as an additional reference point. But this was a most important step, for this conceptual unity of man and his world presupposes that which encompasses both; a Universal Reason which is the ground of both *being* and *knowing*. In man Universal Reason is truly canalized, for, in man, created being and creative knowing combine in an introreflective "gazing into self." It is through this that the transparency of human subjectivity to the order of reason begins to be revealed to man himself.

It remained for the philosophers of the Socratic tradition to draw out the full expanse of meaning implicit in subjectivity turned full round upon itself. Human desire was not regarded by them as a naturally justifiable set of instinctual demands. That physical desire was appropriate to human nature was certainly obvious to them. Plato and Aristotle especially were aware of a sense of fitness in natural desire which gave rise to the concept of *right* as a natural and, correspondingly, also as a legal concept. But *righteousness* was a measure of something else—of subjective rectitude which the main Greek philosophers saw as the proper condition of the soul. Although there was no mortification of the flesh as was the case with many later religions dwelling on man's fallen condition, it was evident in the writings of Plato that he considered the body to be a less than perfect organ as an instrument of Universal Reason. For Plato the soul was Reason's own device for making itself articulate in an existential sense. It was by means of the soul that there could be risked that fallibility which coexists with human freedom. Bereft of the knowing and feeling function of his spiritual self, man would no doubt have followed more closely a routine of behavior similar to that of lower forms of animal life. But if the life of mankind on earth would have been so largely predetermined by a set of instinctive reflexes, it would have been just as unhistorical as that of lower forms of animal life, and just as incapable of self-transcendence.

The history of mankind since its original flourish of ontology and ethical inquiry has made it abundantly clear that the deep perceptive insights of the early Greek scholars did not become a part of the ethical outlook of later civilizations. Indeed, they did not succeed in transforming Athenian culture in which speculative philosophy had been born. The rather rapid shift in the political structure in which Greece became absorbed in an ever-expanding Roman Empire, the budding of early Christianity, and also the marked absence for a long time of any definitive philosophical environment caused philosophical matters to recede from public attention. When philosophical activity entered the post-Renaissance era, most philosophers, with the notable exception of Spinoza and Kant, were concerned with matters other than those of personal rectitude and moral guidance. The general tone was that of keeping abreast of the rising tide of science by paying close attention to methodological criticism and the problem of certainty. But, as the Kantian antinomies were to show, philosophical criticism could become so stringent that it would actually devaluate philosophy as a compelling and final discipline.

For numerous reasons neither the philosophy of the ancients nor that of the modern period has been able to match the precision of science. For one thing, philosophy has always been concerned with a different set of questions. Then also, the kind of success which has been achieved in science has occurred at the price of augmenting the real world. That is, scientific endeavor has always proceeded on the premise that a reductive analysis of phenomena would always be countered by reconciling syntheses of the new data on the part of nonscientific, humanist concerns. After discovering the destructive potential of dynamite, Alfred Nobel established a foundation for the promotion of world peace through humanistic endeavor. But such cases of a man being both a scientist and a humanist philanthropist are indeed rare.

There is no doubt that the method of direct empirical study has thrown considerable light on man's physical and psychological being. It is this which has been the main method and purpose of contemporary naturalist philosophy. But it is also an intrinsic part of the naturalist outlook that everything which is considered must have some direct reference to the physical world. Accordingly, this group of philosophers are concerned with the natural, but not the supernatural, in man. Some of them would go even further and insist that man can be explained completely in physicalist terms and that there is nothing supernatural in man at all. The usual position of the naturalist philosophers is that such matters are beyond the reach of empirical inquiry, and are, therefore, not their concern. It is their professed aim to see man's overt behavior in every possible way that it can be classified, analyzed, and then resynthesized. There are many culture concepts which can be handled this way, from peculiar kinds of musical intonations to the histories of whole civilizations. But what is outside the reach of empirical inquiry is the nature of empirical inquiry itself, for here it is not the observed but the observer that is the problem. Cassirer points out, for example, that whole civilizations can be studied by physical, psychological and sociological categories. "But," he also adds,

the moment we turn from particular works and individuals to the *forms* of culture and abandon ourselves to contemplation of them, we stand on the crest of a new problem. Strict naturalism does not deny the existence of this problem. But it believes itself able to master this "state within a state" by attempting to explain these forms—the forms of language, art and religion—as simple *sum totals* of individual effects. Language is said to be a convention, "something agreed upon," which the individuals simply encounter; political and social life is traced back to a "social contract." The circular nature of such arguments is obvious. For a contract is possible only in the medium of speech, and, similarly, a contract has meaning and force only within a state and medium of laws.[1]

The situation in the study of culture is similar to that in the study of biological man. In both cases there are critical points in their evolutionary development which are lost because what has been achieved has been absorbed in newer media of greater complexity. Consciousness, for example, evolved in man at an incredibly slow rate, and during most of the process, if not all, man was in a prelingual state. Having not yet formulated an adequate symbolism which would lead eventually to the rise of analytic intelligence, consciousness had to depend for its work upon the primary forms of intuitive experience. Therefore, it is not at all surprising to find that interest in intuitive experience has waned considerably, for men are rarely concerned with the various forms of proto-life out of which the forms of real life finally emerged. On the other hand, it should be obvious that it is intuition rather than analytic intelligence which is the real germ of culture. Human culture consists of the sum total of human achievements which can be communicated and reexperienced. But communication can only occur through a set of symbols which holds intellectual designations in place so that their meaning is safely carried from one mind to another. It was intuition which was the ordering element in consciousness—it first evoked the designation of meaning and then by way of symbol gave to each meaning its characteristic sign.

It is, of course, contemporary culture to which one must turn in trying to discover what man's position in the total world process is. But human culture is itself lacking in a fundamental unity. The many different ways in which man uses the power of his mind account for the many different avenues

---

[1] Ernst Cassirer, *The Logic of the Humanities*, p. 108.

of thinking which structures human culture without fitting it into an interlocking whole. The numerous fields of study become separate in the first place because of the numerous ways that man as subject can be affected. What is gathered and conceptually organized in each man can be reduced by rule or principle to the ways of man's functional interaction in set conditions of his physiological or his spiritual environment. There is, for example, the work of analytic intellect which spawned first of all a scientific culture, and then a technology that now, unfortunately, seems to be sweeping civilized humanity toward an unknown and uncertain future. On the other hand there is the work of contemporary intuitive experience which, at its root, not only made technology possible but which builds for itself another world of art, literature and religion. That these convey what is genuinely spiritual in man can be seen in the fact that art cannot have a precise symbolism and still be art, that symbolism in literature is nonanalytic, and that the deeper experiences of religion occur in silence. In no one of these are expression forms reducible to formula description.

What is disturbing is not that man lacks the capacity for inner experience, but rather that the fact and the purpose of this inner experience is so often misunderstood. It comes to be regarded somewhat negatively. That is, inner experience is seldom regarded as an *affirmation* of being, of man's power and capacity to actually transcend the biological nature which he shares with lower animal life and to enter into that reflective experience which is the measure of his true spirituality. Contemplative experience is too often regarded as an escape, as a release from the tensions which technology creates and thrusts upon man. Franz Winkler points out that history is the story of that emancipation by which man shed his dependence on the divine, but in so doing man incurred in its stead a dependence on matter. The ancient prophet or seer may have been helplessly dependent on the supernatural, but modern man is quite unaware that there is anything beyond nature as he encounters it. "Between these extremes," Winkler wrote,

> eras existed when man experienced himself balanced between the ecstacy of the spiritual and the loneliness of material dependence, and these eras are known as the classical periods of history. In them, seeds were planted for the development of that element which stands between Spirit and Nature, the element of human selfhood. Best known to us is the Classical Age of Greece when, in a few individuals at least, there existed a state of balance between intuition and intellect, between temple mystery and natural science, between inner and outer life.[2]

Contemporary man is often captivated by the idea of a technological equivalent of just such a classical age, and the promise of its imminence in his own time. Even though he rejects Marxism as an efficacious means for the fulfillment of a new age of social creativity, contemporary man does seem to share the hope of a universal technological state in which all the desperate needs of mankind will accordingly be satisfied. But neither the Marxists nor those who long only for a technologically perfected culture seem to recognize the hollow victory of a universal state in which man is made to be artificially happy. The twentieth century has witnessed the culmination of another turn which took centuries to complete— a growing alienation of man from his own vibrant inner nature through the stifling process of technological specialization.

What is especially vexing to the coldly analytic philosopher —the philosopher who is himself continuously abreast of an advancing technology—is the fact of spirit in man continuing to encounter itself in paradoxes. No matter how carefully the

---

[2] Franz Winkler, *Man: The Bridge Between Two Worlds* (New York: Harper & Brothers, 1960), p. 160.

determined empiricist tries to exclude spirit from the area of inquiry, it continues to assert itself in all phases of human activity, including the constructing of philosophical systems in which spirit is missing. One may try to smother spirit by reducing its phenomenological appearances to ideas of *function* and the signs of this inner integrity to the *logic* of propositional structures. But this is again the case of the restless ego turning to suspect even itself, and through this suspecting recovering itself in a new dimension of truth. Spirit continuously calls attention to its own estrangement. Man is told that he is lonely, that he has lost his sense of what it is to be intensely human. By immersing himself in the crowd, he tries to recapture some of this lost sense, but he again encounters the same loneliness. The same shrunken world warps even the security of the collective.

It is not the animal in man which is lost, for animal nature is not subject to man's private neurosis. Nor is it a case of man's intellect failing to find its way, for mind simply falls heir to what appears before it. It is the central core in man which senses its abject isolation. This is that specific form of alienation of which Heidegger speaks: the despair of a person who desperately wants to affirm himself by expressing himself in a kind of thinking which is most appropriately his own. His attitude which issues out of this despair rises to the point of defying the traditional ways of representing truth. The alienated person insists that society does not and never has reflected the true nature of man. Socialization is indeed a primitive instinct, but after many centuries, and with numerous advanced instrumentalities of self-expression, human society is still largely geared to herd standards of valuation. Even the technological apparatus which contemporary man so proudly develops is no more than a primitive hut compared with the immense structure of his spiritual being or with the depths of its mystery. It is small wonder that man has become haunted by ego insecurity. It is no wonder that he wants now to reassert his creative personality, to enrich and to reinvigorate society in an entirely new dimension in which the creative vigor of mankind is once more displayed.

One can argue, of course, that this rebelliousness of the ego is nothing more than a sign of ego-inflation; of the ego's failing to accept its own finiteness and its own natural boundaries. But are there such determinable boundaries or does one have to cease talking about the human ego as something which can be easily bounded or defined? Is the human ego, as the Sartrean influence tends to make people believe, something which is condemned by its freedom to a life of despair? Under the Freudian influence the restlessness of the ego was given as an effort to recover the father image which it once knew so well. However, it is not the infantile in man which needs to be awakened, but the full sense of his maturity. Contemporary man is not a badly spoiled child. He is restless, yes, but perhaps because of a good reason.

What haunts modern man more than anything else, and what is perhaps the main source of his ego insecurity, is the threat of a collapse of a warm, personal subjectivity into a cold, lifeless objectification of an external environment. This is more than just a threat as possibility, for the technological invasion of man's private world has already occurred. Technology fulfills man's wants and dreams by mass-produced artifacts, but in doing so it reduces man as worker and producer to the size of the technologically determined slot whereby man fulfills the machine. If the human ego's lack of satisfaction with its own private world is characteristic of a large bulk of human population, then it appears that these private worlds have become abnormally shrunken from their ordinary reach of meaning. The very fact of a host of egoistic centers presupposes a transcendental order of consciousness within which these centers give and receive expression. This transcendental order of consciousness does not imply the existence of some disembodied, super-world ego governing all things by an inflexible and inexorable cosmic will. To suppose such a thing is to fall into the same trap of excessive objectification which is the tendency of a society having an object-centered orientation. Neither is this order of consciousness identical with the totality of being-in-the-world. It is, on the other hand, a vast envelope of subjectivity, of life-forms continually in the process of self-affirmation. It is this transcendental order of consciousness as subjectivity through which concrete *be-ing* is expressed and likewise communicated. As the ground of this *be-ing,* it is creativity in that it is free from the limits of matter and its ultimate conditions. In terms of its substantial effect on a world process continually extending and enlivening itself, universal consciousness is spirit as freedom.

The term *freedom,* however, stands in need of clarification. As a property characteristic of the pressure of a universal *becoming* it is beyond any reference in human knowing. For one thing, human *be-ing* is also to *become,* to *come-to-be* in a universal order of change. For another thing, freedom as absolute spontaneity is outside the kind of cognitive arrest through which human knowing takes place. On the other hand, even though Spirit as consciousness escapes the kind of close-order determination of human cognition, the very act of cognition is itself an essential mark of that fluid consciousness which spreads over and unites human subjectivity in its own kind of nonmaterial bond. Just as the life impulse enters matter in its most unstable forms, so also does Spirit as freedom exert its creative force in its independence from the space-time properties of material reality. As Berdyaev expressed it, "Freedom is creative energy, the possibility of building up new realities." [3]

[3] Nicolas Berdyaev, *The Destiny of Man* (London: Geoffrey Bles, 1937), p. 133.

The problem of a *common* philosophy originates in a concern for the content of freedom. The task of historical philosophy has been to explain the world—the world as *being* or as *knowing,* but in either case the world which surrounds and affects man; and the Marxists added the proviso that, after being explained, the world must be accordingly changed. But there is no changing of the laws of nature; there is no altering possible of the inner laws of particle behavior. Change certainly occurs, but only where there are openings into indeterminacy within structures otherwise highly determinate. The world can be changed according to the Marxist plan only by radically transforming that in which there occurs the largest measure of spontaneity while retaining recognizable properties of deliberate order—human consciousness. What the non-Marxist world regards as a permanent disfigurement of human spirituality is regarded by the Marxists as the triumph of social revolution. For them it is the revolution which is *common.* It is the revolution which bears the truth of history and, therefore, also the truth of man. But philosophy cannot accept this reversal in the order of intelligibility, for history is first of all *human* history which is initially lived and then written by men. It is always man in his freedom who manages to surmount every kind of synthesis intended to confine him to a programmed existence.

It is man's freedom, however, which is problematic. While escaping every form of biological or social determinateness, there is still the matter of its own determination. If man is truly the Logos of society and of history, then man's freedom must be in itself the instrument of a *common* philosophy. That is, it must be that in which the highest form of cosmic reality is expressed. But formulating any kind of philosophical exposition which does justice to man's spirituality while taking into account his existential anchor in animal life is a formidable task. While operating on both levels of spiritual creativity and biotic performance, individual man integrates himself into both, in a voluntary way in one sense and an involuntary in another. In one way he is cosmically predetermined within his possibilities. In the other he is the living presence of a creative force which transcends the boundaries of the first. It is in this mixed condition, with the human ego being solicited by appeals from both directions, that the problem of a common philosophy has to be worked out. It is not a case of man having to be a witness to the empirical world of fact, or even to a transcendent order of faith; but in his having to be a witness to himself; to declare himself fully and completely with regard to what his mission in the world really is. For centuries, and perhaps also for valid reasons, man has nursed a passion for intellectual certitude, which is, in one sense, a sign of spirit having become sunk in an overwhelming concern for ego security. But the human ego cannot be both secure and free; and the price for empirical confirmation is an arrested spirit—one which has come under the domination of something other than itself. It is precisely with regard to human consciousness being concerned with its own existential certainty that the problem of a *common* philosophy becomes alive and real. To be common in the most universal sense of the word, philosophy must embrace the truth of mankind in all man's reaches of being. This involves not only overcoming the polarization of being and knowing as it ordinarily occurs in the cognitive act; it involves coming to terms with man's place in the entire gamut of existential reality. This is a hyperpersonal viewpoint which one can attain only through a heightened perspective of man-in-the-world. But in order to achieve this, it is equally important to understand some things about the-world-in-man.

THE WORLD IN MAN

The two expressions, man-in-the-world and the-world-in-man are not mutually exclusive in content nor are they contrary. They are two reverse sides of the same general concept;

of man having been born in the world carrying the signs of the world's process within himself while elevating this process to a new level of definition. For centuries, the close feelings and the fervent longings of man for union with the mother figure, the Earth, have been played out in numerous mythical and religious themes. Freudian psychology may have exaggerated the maternal idea in explaining psychic complexes, and it may have misread some of the emotional signs with which such complexes became known. But there is an unavoidable attachment of the person to the physical mother with whom he had been for some months in organic union; and because every real physical mother is herself subject to the same set of antecedent influences, it would seem entirely logical to suppose that the maternal influence is deeply embedded as a time deposit in a growing accumulation of psychic unconscious.

The idea of the world-in-man does not rest on any supposed cosmic identity between the basic processes sustaining human life and the basic tensions generated out of the earth itself. Even though the term *human* is derived out of the concept of *humus*, or soil, man is no mere earth figure, but a specialized kind of being whose anterior evolutionary period took millions of years. While the cosmic connections now at work between man as a living organic unit and the life processes in the earth are too obscure for any direct knowing of their immediate relation, there are certain analogue comparisons which can be made. There are evolutionary developmental patterns which abound both in the growth periods of the person and in the cycle of growth and maturation periods of the earth. In both cases there is an energetic system as well as a causal one. An energetic system is one in which there is a kind of energy which underlies every transformation, and, while accounting for the change, it maintains itself as a strong evolutionary pressure until it subsides in a general condition of equilibrium. There are pressures involved in the energy exchange between the sun and the earth which sustain the growing period of plants, but at an appropriate time this energetic system self-converts from a growth to a maturation process. Similarly a part of the libido of a child gestating within the mother's womb is given over to the highly intricate production of a pair of eyes, but the process ends when the eye has reached that stage of perfection when it is an efficacious instrument of sight. It can certainly be granted that the processes in the earth-sun energy direction are certainly not identical with those taking place in a maternal womb, but such a specific implication was never intended. What ought to be clearly understood is that there are certain processes of finality associated with each process, and the nature of the finality process in each case is determined by the particular situation—by the kind of function which the completed organism is to carry out.

One fact which should be understood about the life impulse wherever it exists is that there is always an inner pressure toward existential fulfillment which is indigenous to it. The life impulse is not some substantial entity which can be separated from the mass of matter which it inhabits and be recognized as some intelligible quantum of energy. It is a powerful force whose creativity is mysteriously locked within its own germinal system. In other words, the begetting of life consists originally in the ignition of a particle of matter with life properties by something which is itself alive, and when this ignition occurs the vitalized particle struggles to convert everything palatable and digestible within its reach into its own existential system, and in doing so also struggled to achieve its most articulate kind of performance possibility.

Although the physical performance of life regeneration can be sometimes examined directly, the finality processes which elevate life activities to the active modes of consciousness are not in any way directly knowable. While consciousness in man can be destroyed or made to be ineffectual, it is beyond man's power to deliberately create it in nonconscious material. This power is indigenous to the life process itself. But because the life process works through material realities, it apparently carries with it in its higher instances of creativity some of the residue of the lower. Jung points out that there are unmistakable elements in the collective unconscious which point to influence factors which appear to have some overt connection with conditions in the environmental milieu. He refers to this as the "shadow" within the unconscious. The "shadow" consists of the haunting presence of certain undesirable elements which accumulate because of an unsatisfactory environmental condition. It is, for the most part, a collective representation whose archetype appears under conditions in which mass manifestations of this influence takes place. These archetypes usually appear in times of stress when individual reactions to a threatening social environment become congealed in a mass movement which breaks down all the strength of traditional moral concepts with which man ordinarily fortifies himself. One case which Jung mentions is 1918, when he noticed a peculiar disturbance among his German patients which bore the manifestation of a general inner revolt in the collective unconscious. According to Jung, "it became more and more probable that Germany would be the first victim among the Western nations—victims of a mass movement brought about by the upheaval of forces lying dormant in the unconscious, ready to break all moral barriers." [4]

The critical nature of the problem lies in a conflict of pressures within the psyche complex; between the pressure of a critical reason and that of an uncritical blind passion rooted in the unconscious and composed of elements so wholly irrational that they do not readily surface in consciousness. The

---

[4] C. G. Jung, *Civilization in Transition*, tr. R. F. C. Hull. Bollingen Series XX (New York: Bollingen Foundation, 1946), p. 219.

presence of these elements, however, is not due to any psyche mismanagement or to any congenital defect, but to the fact that human nature quite literally sprang from the soil and that it is still encumbered with traces of the instinctual patterns of the mammalian strain from which man as an erect homo sapiens evolved. Long before man ever became the thinking and responding being which his advanced level of reflective consciousness enabled him to become, there was a ground plan of his instinctual nature which enabled him to cope simultaneously with his inner and outer worlds and to relate the one to the other. While very much man in an anatomical sense, he nevertheless possessed an instinctual sense sharpened by a long period of living close to the earth so that he was in a large sense possessed by the earth. What Jung refers to as the "shadow" in man consists of the archetypes in the collective unconscious which contain and also conceal the instinctual forms of early man which have not been converted into equivalent elements of consciousness. These instinctual forms were remarkably close to the reflexes in animal behavior whose function appears to be that of preserving the individual member against predators of any kind. It is apparently the deep-rooted predator suspicion in man which alarms and arouses him and ignites his antagonistic feelings.

The main difficulty as far as modern man is concerned is not just with the presence of these irrational elements but with the fact that these elements exert their influence in response to situations which only remotely resemble the situations in the primordial era to which these reflexes were intended to react. On the other hand there are conditions in contemporary existence which bring about an upward surge of mass instincts which, in turn, seek some form of collective outlet. The main reason for this upward surge is that people became estranged from their original, primordial laws of natural existence before they managed to amplify human consciousness enough to deal

143

with the most obscure as well as the most obvious forms of human sensitivity. Man has become so highly sensitized to his highly charged social environment that he has all but lost sight of the presence of a primordial kind of psychic consciousness which had its own form of sensitivity. According to Jung,

> Separation from his instinctual nature inevitably plunges civilized man into the conflict between conscious and unconscious spirit and nature, knowledge and faith, a split that becomes pathological the moment his consciousness is no longer able to neglect or suppress his instinctual side. The accumulation of individuals who have got into this critical state starts a mass movement purporting to be the champion of the suppressed. In accordance with the prevailing tendency of consciousness to seek the source of all ills in the outside world, the cry goes up for political and social changes which, it is supposed, will automatically solve the much deeper problem of split personality. . . . What then happens is a simple reversal; the underside comes to the top and the shadow takes the place of light, and since the former is always anarchic and turbulent, the freedom of the "liberated" underdog must suffer Draconian curtailment.[5]

What is the reason for this oppressive presence of collective forces latent within the individual psyche? The force itself is indeed an obscure phenomenon about which the conscious mind can only guess. The fact of the collective, on the other hand, may have an easier and more obvious explanation. Man seems to bear two contradictory elements within himself: a tendency toward individualization and a tendency toward collectivization. On one side there is that inner striving toward individualized, unique existence complete in itself. On the other, there is the threat of ego-insecurity which the person

---

[5] *Ibid.*, p. 289.

144

tries to overcome by reaching or achieving some inner identification with the collective—with the group or crowd—with "society." Jung speaks of a "psychopathic inferiority," a sense of inner insecurity, which attacks psychic consciousness not singly but in large masses. He attributes this to the fact that nations have their own peculiar psychology and therefore also their own particular kind of psychic pathology. As an analogue of Newton's Second Law of Thermodynamics, there seems to be a kind of entropy in human spiritual energy. There is a tendency toward inner relapse—toward a reduction to the elemental and the more instinctual forms, and these achieve their strongest manifestation in the expressions of the collective. The earth, with its multitudinous masses of mineral elements obeying uniformly their own laws of inner properties, is the universal stratum out of which more than one million different organic species have sprung. It is out of this organically creative milieu that a phyletically spiritualized humanity has also sprung. Under the continual force of cosmic evolutionary pressure, mankind is unable to reverse the process even if he wished to do so. Man can deteriorate in the use of his natural functions, but there is no reversing of evolutionary processes. Accordingly he can never look backward—only forward to larger forms of human self-expression. It is no wonder that man's incessant craving for ego-recognition causes him to turn to ideas of the collective; for it is within the collective that he has an unshakable identity. It is for this reason that people cling desperately to their political affiliation, nursing their loyalties with the most arbitrary kind of rationalization.

It is because of the "shadow" in man that large, amorphous, uncontrollable and sometimes unmanageable aggregates of social power grow up by nurturing themselves on feelings of psychopathic inferiority. The principal instance of this case was Nazi Germany. Jung claims to have seen signs of the onrush of the dark forces of the German revolution in the attitudes of his German patients. He claims to have foreseen how these would precipitate in an outburst of mass hysteria. There was, he said, much suffering and destruction, "but when the individual was to cling to a shred of reason, or to preserve the bonds of a human relationship, a new compensation was brought about in the unconscious by the very chaos of the conscious mind." [6] It is for this reason that the German people, reared for centuries in a strong tradition of order, accepted Hitler who was its principal exponent of disorder, and who, according to Jung, "was the most prodigious personification of all human inferiorities." [7]

In his *Lectures on the Philosophy of History,* Hegel points out that, whereas the essence of matter is gravity, that of the spirit is freedom. The dualism which is within man himself— that which accounts for the "shadow"—exists because man embodies both principles within himself. He is forever encumbered with the darkness of matter, and he is far from fully realized as the principle of light in his spirit dimension. The production of ego-consciousness was an unusual evolutionary step, never surpassed or even equalled by anything else in biological life. The restlessness of the ego is a sign of its irrepressible urge toward self-affirmation. The appeal of instinctual satisfaction arises out of a craving for inner identification; the appeal of freedom is the zest for creativity. While there is always the downward thrust of the world-in-man which is the psychic gravity of matter, there is also that buoyant spontaneity of consciousness-in-general. In the first instance there is the urge in man to content himself with that which always falls short of what he seeks; in the second, man is forever enslaved to seeking that which may never be achieved. For a

---

[6] *Ibid.,* p. 230.
[7] *Ibid.,* p. 233.

clearer understanding of either position, it is necessary to turn the inquiry around.

MAN IN THE WORLD

The idea of man-in-the-world has become a matter of special concern for anthropology, sociology and history mainly because it is man's "in-the-worldness" which reveals him in the fullest dimension of his being. In practically every case the tone of the inquiry seems to indicate that the process of human development is irreversible; that while there may be recurrent situations, there is no recreating of the past. Human development invariably entails a continual eruption into what is often unexpected and unforeseen. Because the methods used by investigators in any area are essentially reductive, proceeding from complex affairs to simpler ones, the investigators are always assured of some empirical certainty. But there is also an unavoidable hazard in reductive analysis. When data which has simply filtered through an amorphous mass of detail is allowed as evidence there is always the risk that the underlying synthesis of the whole phenomenon may become lost. While the need for a synopsis outlook may not be an urgent matter in every case, there are many instances in which a general reference matrix is important. In human affairs, for example, the breadth and depth of concern has increased in the past century from what was almost totally a system of ethnic solidarities to one of global interest. In this case the world outlook has improved mainly in a quantitative respect; the human vision has been extended to include an awareness of more nations and many more millions of people, but without any significant deepening of concern. Further, in social research, as in other fields, the demand for technical efficiency always seems to require that the empirical scientific method be closely adhered to. On the other hand the need for a qualitative outlook, or *Weltanschauung,* has not greatly impressed very many scholars, mainly perhaps because maintaining a wider outlook entails the risk of losing one's sense of inner security. As Carl Gustav Jung pointed out:

> There are many scientists who avoid having a Weltanschauung because this is supposed not to be scientific. It has obviously not dawned on these people what they are really doing. For what actually happens is this: by deliberately leaving themselves in the dark as to their guiding ideas they cling to a lesser, more primitive level of consciousness than would correspond to their true capacities. Criticism and skepticism are not always a sign of intelligence—often they are just the reverse, especially when used by someone as a clock to hide his lack of Weltanschauung.[8]

Although a Weltanschauung, as Jung uses it, is something which occurs on the level of consciousness, he locates the roots of this outlook in man in the entire composition of the human psyche. He points out that the presence of an archaic layer in the human unconscious indicates the presence of a historical collective. Although mankind has spread itself over the whole face of the earth, there is a certain amount of racial history and tradition implanted within the psychic make-up of the single person. The picture Jung puts together of the human story is that of living, cohesive racial or ethnic wholes which stretch far back into the primordial origins of psychic consciousness and which were carried forward by a timeless and eternal world process.

In order to involve itself with the entire range of its concern, philosophy must ultimately involve itself with the noosphere—with the works of culture—with that which reveals

---

[8] Carl Gustav Jung, *The Structure and Dynamics of the Psyche* (New York: Bollingen Foundation, 1960), p. 362.

mankind to itself at its highest level of spiritualization. It must also involve itself in the task of recognizing the succession of modes through which human life is graduated from one style of existence to another. But a knowledge of man's historical evolution requires much more than just an analysis of his biological progress. When one examines the artifacts which he fashioned—first the crude stone implements of the Neolithic period; later the carved frescoes on tombs and walls; still later the primitive art by which man was becoming more articulate in symbolization; and then the work of the artisan fashioning intricate and delicate pieces of pottery and jewelry—some insight is gained into the progressive increase in manual dexterity which took many centuries to develop. This was an indication of the morphological side of man as a being who was able to invent and to use tools. Tool-making was the step which started him on the way to a life far above animal existence. The older tools were fashioned in accordance with the requirements of man's physical existence, and a very important by-product of these was a surplus of free social energy which man could then deploy in a new direction of effort. Eventually man utilized this surplus of free time and energy to improvise a new tool system which was connatural with himself—a system of language, or oral and written communication.

With the use of articulate symbolization and expression, the hominoid species emerged from within its evolutionary cocoon at a rate much faster than ever before. How far back this period of evolutionary development goes is difficult to tell, but it is quite likely that it had its roots deep in the Neolithic period in which the earliest artifacts depicting human self-expression are noted. But the accuracy with which modern man is able to read the message of his own antiquity is another question. Perhaps modern intellectual sentiment lacks an awareness that human consciousness ripened very slowly.

For one thing, an all too literal reading of Genesis has led modern man to think of himself as a product of instantaneous creation—of Adam and Eve being truly the very first humans —the real progenitors of the human race, able to speak and to be conversant not only with a serpent but also with God. One of the side effects of the modern intellectual assault upon the natural environment is that every kind of human message has to be interpreted and evaluated in terms of scientific accuracy and credibility and that man's critical evaluation of his own evolutionary history has to be made in an empirically verifiable manner. It is for this reason that the modern intellectual tends to be contemptuous of some of the writings of the past as if these were written in the childhood period of consciousness. But this only points out that it is contemporary intellectualism which is itself naive in being unable to grasp the message which cultural antiquity had no choice but to express in mythological terms. Even today's language is rich in metaphor, such as that which pervaded the early Biblical texts and much of the rhetoric describing tribal mystery and festival. The passage in Genesis 3:7 "And the eyes of them were opened, and they knew that they were naked" could hardly be taken in the literal sense of their both being physically blind. For the very use of the term "naked" presupposes an understanding on their part of the difference between being clothed and unclothed. Similarly, the story about the youths protecting Zeus from his "child-eating" father was not the kind of sensationalism to which the Western mind is accustomed, but rather a rhetorical figure intended to carry the message of a budding intellectualism having to be made secure. The father's name in this case was Cronos, which was the Greek word for time. This is the clue which enables the more perspicacious Western minds to read the message correctly. Zeus was the Olympian deity from whom had sprung the gods of learning and culture. For many centuries human experience had been eroded by time. In time things appeared, but also disappeared. Until there developed an articulate symbolism, there were but few ways through which the meaningful elements of such experience could be held in place. The Olympian deities were neither disembodied entities hovering over mankind, nor were they merely the result of later writers' fantasies. They represented the slowly developing powers in man's own intellect which were beginning to influence and transform him inwardly, and to set him on a new course of evolutionary growth. Symbol and language thrust humanity in an entirely new direction. Once man had set himself on this road, his intellectual appetites and heuristic drives were kindled to a new pitch. Time was no longer something which absorbed all of man's energies in a tangential encounter with the world. Simple tool-making was ebbing, and instrumentation was beginning to be born. Man was now learning how to reconstruct his ideas and express them as symbolic truth.

One early result of the growth of language was a kind of social conviviality which had been all but impossible before. Conviviality had been one of the early signs of psychogenesis which had been organizing one new life form upon another. There was, for example, the bare form of conviviality which was indigenous to the clustering of cells: *symbiosis,* or life in common. This kind of collective inhabitation persisted through the whole extension of psycho-genesis from an early, primitive kind of clustering throughout the gradual and extensive metamorphosis of thousands of species springing from a single strain. But conviviality on the level of human experience is a far different phenomenon. It operates on the principle of spiritual rather than energetic tension. Far more volatile than the assortments of protein molecules which comprise the various biological structures, conviviality on the level of consciousness undergoes numerous instances of dissolving and of being reformulated within a brief interval of time. The random, free association of humans is set in motion by a set of energetic tensions generated from within each person and placed in operation by an articulate framework of language.

Definite forms of sociality tend to occur whenever two requisite conditions are met. The first one is, of course, the copresence of an articulate system of communication through which men are able to recognize and realize their heuristic passions in directions conducive to their fulfillment. Their fulfillment, however, presupposes some internal standard by which the value of heuristic endeavors take on some existential signification. The second condition is, therefore, a commitment to a definite kind of moral idealization. Taken together, these two reveal something of the homogeneity of mankind all over the earth. Chardin points out that the totum which is mankind can shift and bend in numerous ways because of the extraordinary elasticity of mankind as a zoological group. Even though mutations are continually produced and different races have come into existence under special climatic and geographic influences, the many branches remain as offshoots of one main trunk. "Zoologically speaking," Chardin says,

> mankind offers us the unique spectacle of a "species" capable of achieving something which all previous species have failed. It has succeeded, not only in becoming cosmopolitan, but in stretching a single organized membrane over the earth without breaking it.[9]

What is indeed unique in the human situation is the intensity with which the psychic web has stretched as a membrane over the earth. It is possible to think of the entire gamut of processes in the world as fitted into a matter-energy system; a system wherein matter is continually being trans-

---

[9] Pierre Teilhard de Chardin, *The Phenomenon of Man* (New York, Harper & Brothers, 1959), p. 241.

formed in a precise way by a set of energy tensions appropriate to an internal design. But man-in-the-world makes a displacement of his being upon it. This is not the slow, exploratory movement of spirit resident in biotic evolution but an advanced condition of spirit *qua* human consciousness releasing its ebullience upon what it has already created. There is an absolute difference between the world and man-in-the-world which cannot be overcome by any naturalist philosophy description of either one. The difference is consciousness-in-general, which is spirit in its most advanced form of truth being for itself. Animal consciousness is a participation of consciousness-in-general, but only as it is befitting to animal nature and to the collective realization of the species. One can go even further by saying that there is an enhanced form of animal consciousness in the form of an animal community. But the sense of community among animals or among insect species is an advanced form of collective preservation of biological capacity. There is no apparent breakthrough to a self-sustaining truth-for-itself. There is no animal culture—no articulate symbolism serving as an instrument for consciousness-in-general which is appropriate to animal consciousness and expression. It is only on the level of humanity that the self-sustaining, energetic aspects of truth-for-itself reveal themselves as consciousness-in-general constantly clarifying itself. That is, this is not just the tangential encounter of human consciousness shaping itself in accordance with the world as outer presentation. It is also this same consciousness coming to terms with its own inner reality. It is in this sense that the large difference between the mere collective and the community ought to be made clear. The collective is an aggregate which is formed in order to serve as an instrument of external order; the community is a viable existence form of man's social nature in which the function is the expansion of human truth. As Berdyaev expressed it,

There is an absolute difference between the life of community on the one hand and collectivism on the other. The former is a brotherly community in Truth on the part of human beings whose freedom is an accepted fact. Collectivism on the other hand is a compulsory organization of the community, it is the recognition of the collective as a special kind of reality which stands above human personality and oppresses it by its authority. Community life is the effective realization of the fullness of the free life of personalities. . . . Collectivism on the other hand is the degeneration and disfigurement of human thought and conscience, it is the alienation of thought and conscience, it puts man into subjection to a fictitious and unauthentic reality.[10]

The tension between the sense of community and that of collectivization occurs within the community itself. It also occurs within a bare collective struggling to become community, where its truth would become more perfectly realized. This is not a societal phenomenon; it is rather something which occurs within man himself—an epiphenomenon of conscience which is a kind of tension, as Kierkegaard expressed it, between divine and human freedom. It is a tension which the pragmatist and the logical positivist philosopher try desperately to ignore. And while the humanist philosopher is touched inwardly by it he too tries to deal with it in an empirical and coldly analytic manner. Human freedom is not a condition of pure creativity. With regard to his freedom, modern man's condition is very similar to that of Adam in the Garden of Eden; it is forever subject to the world as objectively realized. It is forever tempted to accept the objectively frozen world—that which has become creatively inert—as its main reference guide. According to Berdyaev, objectization of

---

10 Nicolas Berdyaev, *Truth and Revelation* (London: Geoffrey Bles, 1953), p. 25.

any kind is a fall. It is a relapse of spirit because it has allowed itself to come under forms which are creatively inactive and unproductive. Spirit, on the other hand, is pure creativity. In extending itself in creation, Spirit submits to limitations in being and in space-time location. That is, in being creative through the use of concrete materials, it is bound by the limitations which materials under space-time conditions impose. Because man embodies this polarity of creativity and limitation within himself, his creative aspirations are subject to internal frustrations. Creativity in man, for example, entails the urge toward community, but the movement toward community often converts into a movement toward collectivization. The reason is that, while the sense of community is something which is only inwardly realized, man continually rationalizes his existential condition, and in doing so he creates the collective as a social image of himself. It is for this reason that Plato's *Republic* could never actually resemble a politically existing and active state. It is an ideal of human community, described, unfortunately, in some cases with terminology which had a metaphorical rather than a literal intent. Johann Fichte's first idea of the state as a community of free individuals bore the same sense of ideality. But Fichte's progressive development of the state as an articulate social organ causes it to be a nearly totalitarian organ in which the sense of the personal in the community had disappeared almost altogether.

The problem of man-in-the-world is one which has to be recognized in terms of concepts which are appropriate to it— concepts which come closer than any others in conveying man's existential condition. While the account in Genesis of man's fall into sin may not be factually true, it is a metaphor concerning man's condition which ought not to be ignored. For one thing, man's spiritual capacity is clearly evident. The Fall is something which could only happen to man, since it is only man who is capable of making a moral decision. A second thing is that the Fall resulted from man's own natural condition; it was no divine or cosmic accident. Because man's natural condition was in a physical sense very much the same as it is now, and was in the interim period, the Fall is something which modern man must experience himself. Like man in the Sartrean sense being condemned to be free and to make choices, modern man cannot escape the voice of conscience and the pressure upon his mind of consciousness-in-general. Man can no more avoid his freedom than he can avoid thinking or having moral sensibilities. Accordingly his participation in consciousness-in-general forces him to accept the tragic as part of his existence.

To understand the meaning of the existentially tragic, one has to take the concept of tragedy out of its temporal and experiential setting. The tragic is more than just what happens to someone under unfortunate circumstances. It is the presence and the force of nonbeing which is always attached to *being,* and the existential place of the tragic can only be understood when considered against the background of eschatology. In its naturalistic sense, "eschatological" refers to things which are final in the order of cosmic or historical law. But eschatology *per se* does not contain that which is given in naturalistic terms since it deals with that which occurs both outside of, and at the culmination, of historical time. It refers to the time when things capable of eternity are to be made permanent or eternal. But an eschatology does not occur except with the simultaneous occurrence of an apocalypse. An apocalypse is a death of the cosmos. It is a sweeping away of all which is imperfect and impure. One forms some idea of this when one considers the debris of dying civilizations which is swept away in the tragic course of violent social change. But an apocalypse cannot be explained in rational terms. While one thinks of it as occurring at the end of time, the end of time contributes nothing to the apocalypse. The paradox of the eschatological, therefore, can never be resolved by the use of naturalist symbols. Even though naturalist symbols have reference to life and growth, they inevitably also entail concepts of death and destruction. Eschatology, on the other hand, embraces only that in which the fullness of being is accomplished and is forever retained. Accordingly, it can never be conceived of in a time dimension. While the concept has meaning only in terms of man's creative spirituality, mankind will never participate in the eschatological moment, but only in the movement toward it. A philosophy of mankind is, accordingly, a philosophy of what transpires in an interim of the Absolute. Man's being-in-the-world—is God's highest moment of self-estrangement, not yet in full recovery of Himself. Eschatology is the end of the self-estrangement. It is also the completion of man's creative self-actualization. Human self-estrangement is something of an analogue of the Divine going-out-of-self. The point which should be made clear for either case is that spiritual self-estrangement is not something which is merely negative. Its negativity arises from a reduced power of self-affirmation; not that of deliberate self-alienation. There is, moreover, the positive side of self-estrangement—its power of creativity. Being creative entails a loosening of the hold of objectivization. That part of the world which is forever objectively certain is never in any way existentially separated from itself. It is entirely secure from any loss of being. On the other hand, it likewise lacks the power of existential ascent.

That man not only has but exercises the power of existential ascent is evident in the fact of his creative and also self-actualizing power. The most tangible signs of this power of creative advance are the many manipulative devices with which man has brought the empirically objectified world under his management and control. But in his passion for existential security there is one problem which has persistently escaped solution—man's own social nature. To be sure, his *social* nature is not radically different from his personal one. The point is that, while man's most extravagant forms of ill intent are carried out under social conditions, these conditions confuse and distort man's own problem. For one thing they are the occasion of one form of ill intent—that in which man rejects problems indigenous to his own nature and attaches them to something called "society." Society is man's own form of self-objectification. Although it is a mirror reflection of collective mankind, what is caused to reflect and what is seen as existing are often widely different. The fact is that man does not really see himself at all, but rather some collective representation of mankind which has to be continually rationalized in legal terminology. The *good* in man is somehow converted into a *good law*. On the other hand, there are the chronic ills of the collective which cause its continual deterioration. Human personality which is the disclosure of the image of God in man is somehow carefully and systematically removed from the fields of law, of economics, of history—and even from that secular discipline which is presumed to be closer to actual human nature than any other—sociology. Man continues to be a problem to himself because he refuses to take that inward step toward self-analysis. Rather than face himself in an inner self-confrontation, he attempts to set the problem entirely on the plane of the psychology of the collective. The goal of legislative action is in keeping with the herd standards by which social assessments are made: a reasonably well-ordered system which shapes and regulates human behavior as a whole while leaving enough open prerogatives to satisfy all levels of human desire.

The process of making human society a concrete, living reality by way of a progressive refinement of a legal system is a mark both of man's success in objectifying himself socially and of his failure to achieve the same level of social behavior through his own spiritual self-awakening. Through the act of baptism a person becomes committed to that spiritual community which is the Kingdom of God, and the act of commitment is done by the parents and sponsors or by the person himself. Man's membership in that earthly kingdom which is human society requires no act of contrition nor any declaration of faith or moral intent. Accordingly the conscience levels on which man functions in the social milieu are assessed or measured in terms of what a collective good is, which is, in turn, unavoidably utilitarian. Being utilitarian is not in itself lacking in intrinsic goodness; it involves a lack of that particular kind of goodness which is the measure of man's spiritual growth rather than what meets or satisfies his practical needs. This is not a condition which is indigenous to man's spiritual situation in the twentieth century. It is something which is traceable to the entire growth period of human wisdom and conscience. The fact that this is not revealed in the kind of literal language which modern man has learned to respect does not obviate the fact that there are other kinds of messages which man can ill-afford to ignore. The myths of antiquity, for example, are not the kind of idle fantasy which one often imagines they are. They often contain metaphors which are highly revealing of the long and sometimes interrupted periods of the growth of man's deeper sense of conscience; in fact, even of the awakening of human conscience itself. It would be foolish, for example, to pass off the myth of Agamemnon as merely the tale of a wicked adulteress and her lover who ultimately receive their just punishment, and whose wickedness also brought on insanity in her son who had to avenge his father's death as a matter of tribal justice. That Orestes was driven insane by the strange visions which haunted him is certainly part of the story, and by the standard of man's normal emotional condition that is certainly regrettable. The point, however, which a literal reading of the tale is likely to miss altogether, is that Orestes was *innocently guilty*. The term *innocent* refers to his moral condition under the old code of tribal justice whereby good or evil was a function of the social condition of the whole rather than of man's own personal condition. The term *guilty* was a new one when taken in a personal sense, for it signified a new stage in man's moral development; one in which man became personally imputable for his spiritual misdeeds and answerable to a spiritual kingdom which transcends any collective representation of himself which man is able to make. The terribly confused mental condition of Orestes signified that he bore within himself the transition trauma of the passing from one stage to another. By blood and by historical circumstance he belonged to the older one, and his whole routine of life was determined for him without any choice on his part. On the other hand, his growing sense of internal conscience makes it plain that choice, and especially moral choice, was becoming more and more a part of man's natural situation. Finally, the act of atonement which Orestes had to perform after having been acquitted by a jury of gods and men was a sign of the highly positive side of man's moral state in that man must, through his own efforts and in suffering and sorrow, build for himself a spiritual kingdom on earth.

Although the tale of Orestes was supposed to signify a new upward surge in man's inner intuitive sense, this sharpened intuitionism was itself giving rise to a growing intellectualism which would also achieve a peak in the ethical climate of Greek antiquity. By this time, however, hardened forms of social politics had appeared which managed to stifle human self-enlightenment in many ways. While Greek philosophers could speak and write about the agapé potential of the free citizen, free citizenship as such was conferred on but a fortunate few, and slavery was accepted as a very natural part of the social condition. The collapse of the system which occurred with the growing decadence of the Roman Empire was a strong piece of testimony that man's spiritual kingdom on earth was not something which could be legalistically engineered. The tale of Orestes—representing an epoch in approximately the eighth century B.C.—marked the period of inner growth of man's conscience as an individual. It left no sign or direction by which this growing sense of right could transform a whole society; how it could ignite a collective of itself with the fire of spiritual inner-rejuvenation. Moreover, the heavenly clock was drawing to the point of striking a new hour as the age of Aries which had dominated so much of the Achaean growth period was coming to an end. A new period in history was beginning to dawn, one which would be heralded by the simplest of figures—the Shepherds of Judea.

THE CHRISTIAN EXPECTATION

The incarnation of Truth in the person of Christ was a break—a most significant one—with the power of objectification. What is also important in this case is that the break occurred by way of objectification, for Christ was indeed man in the flesh. By immersing Himself in the concrete order of nature, Christ the man-God overcame existential estrangement. In telling His disciples "I have overcome the world," He made it clear that the power of material objectification was no longer the final commanding power on earth as far as man was concerned. The power of the concrete forces of nature were by no means destroyed. The redemptoriness of Christianity was not that of rescuing the faithful by removing them from the natural world, nor that of removing evil from the world. Redemption meant restoring man in the eternal order of God, but it meant also redeeming *man in the world;* of causing man to be able to overcome within himself the forces of temptation from which he had been shielded by a strict observance of the law. The salvation of man is not something which is accomplished when man is removed from the area of temptation. The power of personal redemption is something which man can experience directly and which calls for his personal participation. For the Jewish prophets and their followers, obedience to the law of justice and righteousness had been the way of reaching God. But now the power of estrangement between God and man and between man and man, which had made problematic the fulfillment of the law of justice and righteousness as the only approach to God, was removed. "To experience the New Being in Jesus as the Christ," wrote Paul Tillich, "means to experience the power in him which has conquered existential estrangement in himself and in everyone who participates in him." [11] The law, St. Paul wrote in Galatians 3, had been the tutor in bringing man to Christ. "There can be neither Jew nor Greek, there can be neither bond nor free, there can be no male and female; for ye all are one *man* in Christ Jesus. And if ye are Christ's, then are ye Abram's seed, heirs according to promise."

The incarnation of Christ in human flesh left its mark as a refocus of history, both in time and in terms of historical meaning. But the refocus itself is not always understood. Just where does the figure of Christ fit in with the historical continuity of spirituality in mankind? Where is the reconciliation between the cast of mind which is ideal from the point of view of ethics and psychology, and that of religion, especially Christianity? For those who have been reared in the Christian tradition, the reconciliation resides immanently in the figure of Christ, who, as the Logos of the world, invested Himself organically with the world, and in so doing overcame the physical meaning of death. That this attitude may be a natural Christian prejudice is, of course, true. But one ought at least

---

[11]Paul Tillich, *Systematic Theology* (Chicago: The University of Chicago Press, 1957), II, 125.

extend the inquiry far enough to see whether there are any really unifying aspects of Christ's presence on earth which stand out unmistakably, apart from personal bias.

That there were a number of prophets in Old Testament history is certainly the case. It is also true that they were called prophets because of their unusual insights and perceptive powers. If one may accept the accounts of what they did in a literal sense, they did perform wondrous things. The main question, however, is whether Christ was really God in the flesh, the true Messiah, or one prophet among many others. The fact that Christ was born a Jew might lead one to think that the latter must have been the case. But if one takes that point into consideration, then it is equally as important to look further into the history of the Jewish people.

In being born a Jew, Christ was a link in the long history of a people who had gone through a long period of growing intuitive consciousness of God's love and mercy for all people.

"The Jews," wrote Franz Winkler, "were the chosen people because they were the first to look beyond the powers working in nature to the higher aspect of God as pure spirit." [12] They had maintained before Moses a long tradition of monotheism. They also had the unusual capacity of enduring the suffering which was laid upon them. No other race has shown such a capacity for spiritual growth springing from long periods of intense oppression.[13] In Winkler's view, suffering and

---

[12] Franz Winkler, *Man: The Bridge Between Two Worlds* (New York, Harper & Brothers, 1960), p. 76.

[13] According to Edwin A. Burtt, an answer to the question of the suffering of the Jews is given by Second Isaiah. "The terrible calamity which the Jews had suffered, he is sure, is not a proof of special guilt on their part but rather of a specially exalted role that Yahweh is calling them to fill. Hence it is not a sheer evil (as would be the case were it nothing more than punishment for past sin) but an experience that can be turned to a new, hopeful, creative use—for them and for the entire world. If taken aright, it can purge them of the proud, self-centered vices that had corrupted them in the past—it

sorrow had become the lot of God's Chosen, not for their having committed more grievous errors than others, but because they were the ones who were capable of recognizing the spiritual meaning of tragedy and distress, and of taking upon themselves the task of leading others to the truth of Yahweh's religion.

In being born born in Bethlehem, Christ fulfilled the expectations of those to whom it had been foretold that a scion of the house of David would at some date be born, and that He would have supernatural powers which no force on earth could resist. In this way He fulfilled the Messianic expectation born of ancient Hebrew origin, and also the contribution of the Hebrew people to world history. One can argue, of course, that the rejection of Christ by the Jews cancels out any fitting of Christ into their historical design. However, that is not really the case, for what one is concerned with is whether anyone claiming to be the Messiah and who is acclaimed to be the Messiah is born on earth and appears to men. The Jewish contribution to messianic hope lies in the fact that this message is born in suffering and unhappiness, and it awaits the day of messianic triumph. Other than just rejecting Christ as the Messiah, the Jews may have misunderstood His role in history. But that would not be so very surprising, for many of the early Christians did not understand it very well either.

In order to understand the messianic message, one must

---

can point the way toward the achievement of a new national personality, moved by novel aspirations and ideal purposes, and embodying a power of self-giving that was previously beyond them. . . . Although it was an overwhelming evil when it came upon them, their tragic defeat was a necessary preparation for a unique spiritual role —the role of serving as a light to the nations, of atoning for the sins of the world as well as their own, of founding an era of universal peace and brotherhood under Israel as teacher and guide." Edwin A. Burtt, *Man Seeks the Divine* (New York: Harper & Row, 1957), p. 327.

recognize, first of all, its eschatological character. Messianic hope is not the hope of inwardly transforming the world. It is, of course, because of the nature of the world and of objectification that the Messianic message is given at all. That is, it is a hope which is for the recovery of inwardness. Accordingly, the gospel of the Messiah can be received only by those who are capable of comprehending its message—the message of a personal recovery from the world, of overcoming the existential estrangement which is man's lot. It is charismatic in its outlook, and as such it is also irrational in terms of the prevailing ideas and levels of speculation. However, because it is a message aimed at man-in-the-world, it is also necessarily involved with tragedy, and it must necessarily involve itself with the tragic in existence.

In His death on the cross, Christ brought into focus the universal meaning of suffering and its atoning power. In being born a Jew He stood as one who was born under the law; it was his heritage to be subject to it. But in submitting Himself to it He also fulfilled the law by achieving a completion of its meaning. In setting Himself up against the officials of the Sanhedrin, He made it clear that His purpose was not to bring the Jewish religion to its historical termination; that his role as Savior was not to nullify the law, but to fulfill its task of redeeming man-in-the-world.

What has happened, meanwhile, to the saving message of spiritual creativity which Christianity is supposed to bring? Where is the transforming power which the world now seems to need so urgently? For two possible reasons the effects of the intense, spiritual personalism of Christ have become sharply lowered. One is the fact that the message of Christianity is disclosed only through the work of vibrant, living personalities who are willing to take up the cross and assume the missionary zeal of St. Paul. The other fact is that there has arisen a tendency in Christianity to make Christ's message take on the character of a moral legalism. Instead of "fulfilling the law," it becomes another law.

The moral aims of Christianity were often misunderstood even by some of its most faithful adherents. For in coming to redeem man-in-the-world, the world itself had to sometimes appear unattractive, as if it were evil in itself and the source of everything evil. St. Augustine's City of the World, the City of Babylon, was the world's social condition. Accordingly the State was necessary for a negative reason—it was an instrument of order for something which was in a fallen condition. It was very difficult, if not impossible, for St. Augustine to reconcile this negative role of the State with the positive transforming power of Christianity. For other early Christians as well, the core of Christianity was to be more and more separated from the world outside so that the gap between saint and infidel would be more and more unbridgeable. Consequently, there was no constructive vision of the world in a Christian sense. "Had the fire of early Christianity," wrote Winkler,

> been permitted to draw fuel from pagan wisdom, its glow might have endured and given rise to a truly constructive science and a civilization of world-wide brotherhood. Since it did not, religion lost its foundations in earthly life and science its moral aims. The medieval church, recognizing the dangers but not their cause, felt she had to protect man from his own pre-mature intellectualism, and retard the progress of science.[14]

Where does Christianity stand in relation to a common philosophy? One main requirement of a philosophy which is presumed to be *common* is that it be deeply involved in existential experience, for it is here that one encounters the given

---

[14] *Ibid.*, p. 194.

as spiritual creativity. It was for this reason that there was such a dedication of spiritual passion among the early Christians. "Originally," Winkler wrote, "the strongest motive for Christian charity was compassion for Christ. What one did for the least of men, one did for the Son of God who shared the sufferings of all humanity." [15] But this passion seems to have been retarded by a blind adherence to the world. According to Winkler,

> The alchemists went a step further. They felt that God had given part of His self not only to living and conscious beings, but to *dead matter* as well. There it lay imprisoned to await deliverance through creative deeds of man. Man, in turn, could regain his lost vision of God only by his compassionate love for the divine in nature. Compassion for the Savior made hundreds of thousands take up the cross, gave unearthly beauty to medieval mysticism, and inspired the mysterious legends of the Holy Grail. It found expression in Richard Wagner's *Parsifal* which reveals the message of the Grail in the drama's final words: "Miracle of highest grace: redemption for the Redeemer." [16]

How does the message of Christianity fit into an interlocking picture of human history and development, especially insofar as it is a fertilizing principle of a common philosophy? Regardless whether one accepts and professes the Christian faith or not, one cannot ignore the impact which its message has had upon post-Hellenic civilizations. One can no more disregard this than one can disregard the far-reaching influence of Buddha and Confucius in Far Eastern culture.

A *common* philosophy is, first of all, a philosophy of man and of his experience. More precisely it is a philosophy of

---

[15] *Ibid.*, p. 232.
[16] *Ibid.*, p. 232.

man *in* his experience. Existentialism, modern humanism, philosophical naturalism—and even logical positivism—all touch directly upon man and his nature. Essentially, the concern in every case is for some vital sense of the *being* of man. The philosophical naturalist sees man in terms of his homogeneousness with nature—with the living, pulsating forces of the organic world and its inner processes. Man has been factually created to be a part of this world, and by means of one's knowledge of the whole of nature, man, the naturalist contends, can be factually understood. The humanist is apparently deeply sensitive to the more striking emotional currents and feelings within man, and these are the root of the inner values which, it is hoped, will come to light in a humanist intellectualism. The existentialist, on the other hand, looks at man's more extroverted outpourings, man's apparent feelings of deep despair and anxiety, and he tries to formulate these into some coherent existentialist analysis of man's condition. Finally the logical positivist, at least on the surface unconcerned with the phenomenology of human existence, confines himself to the small inner recess of man's power of being —his logical formulations.

In a more direct and precise sense, the common philosophy is human subjectivity. That is, philosophy is *common* when it is most nearly identical with man's being; when it reveals man directly in terms of his power of spiritual creativity. Creativity is spirit as energy, as energy flowing freely out of man's power of being. But man's power of being involves being-in-the-world, and this inevitably entails engaging oneself with the tragic inherent in human existence. The tragic is something which occurs only within the domain of Spirit. It occurs when Spirit, moving to be whole, encounters the self-destructiveness which is part of the world of material objectification; a world which is run on the simpler, but inexorable, terms of entropy and energy reduction. Subjectivity is itself a case of spirit moving to be whole. That this is a kind of humanism is quite true, but it is not that type of "scientific" humanism whereby the approach to subjectivity is a coldly analytic objective detachment. It is more a radical humanism in which there is a compassionate engagement of oneself with what is encountered; it is a remaking of the engagement into a genuine spiritual reality so that it is obviously and ostensibly a victory for subjectivity. The clue to the meaning of this victory is sacrifice. Sacrifice in this case is neither some routine symbolic gesture nor some ostensible means of appeasing a wrathful God. It means literally to give oneself up; to hand oneself over and to be at the disposal of fate. It is in this sense that the Christian message has to be received to be understood. The figure of Christ is that of the New Being; that which is capable of taking the existential estrangement of mankind upon Himself; and, by overcoming death, overcoming also the worst kind of existential estrangement that can happen to man. A significant point, however, and one which is so easily missed is that what is being handed over is not what is final in itself, but that which is itself corruptible, despite its existential appeal. But handing over what is existentially appealing requires a special kind of spiritual courage. It involves a complete resignation of being in the ordinary sense, with full confidence that in the New Being one's own being is also restored.

In what way does the idea of existential estrangement become an intrinsic part of the whole idea of mankind on earth? The whole tradition of estrangement seems to be derived from the concept of the Fall, which, unfortunately, has been treated as an accidental lapse into a sinful, evil condition. This is unfortunate because it exaggerates the idea of the condemnation of mankind by a wrathful God while it deemphasizes the whole idea of Spirit in man as creativity. It makes it appear as if the creativity implanted in man had no other function than to continually acquiesce in, or to be a kind of, ontic reflection of Divine creativity without any personal participation on man's part. It also makes it appear as if man's freedom, as an accessory condition of the Fall, amounted to a negation of the divine image in man. Both of these positions miss the central idea of freedom as creativity. The Divine analogue involved in both freedom and creativity does not permit any exact transfer from man to God or vice-versa. But some clarification can still be made. The term *creature* presupposes an ultimate in creation—that which is in itself creative. According to Paul Tillich,

> In maintaining that the fulfillment of creation is the actualization of finite freedom we affirm implicitly that man is the *telos* of creation. Of no other being that is known can it be said that finite freedom is actualized within it. In other beings there are preformations of freedom such as Gestalt and spontaneity, but the power of transcending the chain of stimulus and response by deliberation and decision is absent.[17]

The concept of freedom as creativity has been lost because of an excessive concern in the modern world for empirical results—for values which have some tangible reference to man as a sensuous being. Freedom has come to derive its meaning as an escape from the stringent hold which a mechanized society lays upon everyone caught in its particular kind of mesh. Freedom as creativity, however, is something more than the feeble sense of life of an almost extinguished subjectivity. Creativity is an affirmation of being and, as Tillich also points out, "being a creature means both to be rooted in the creative ground of the divine life and to actualize one's self through freedom. Creation is fulfilled in the creaturely self-realization

---

17 Tillich, *Systematic Theology*, I, 258.

which simultaneously is freedom and destiny." [18] Also, creativity is an outpouring of oneself—a moral act which is manifest in the work of conscience as the product of man's heuristic passion. Heuristic passion is a drive toward fulfillment. The binding effect of this passion is a mark of the transcendence of the human spirit. It unites without enforcing rigid space-time connections. It unifies without altering the fundamental composition of what is brought into the circle of unification. It overcomes in various ways the self-dichotomizing tendencies inherent in a way of existence which often exalts individuality as one of its highest goods.

What is required to complete the concept of man as spiritual creativity is the concept of human love. To be sure, love is private and personal, and it is known and experienced mainly through the emotions. Also, love is irrational from the standpoint of the legislation of reason. Reason is a kind of intellectual compulsion, and love and compulsion are antithetical to each other. But if love is so far removed from rational analysis, how can it be a legitimate issue for philosophy?

The ambiguous place of love in philosophy is due to the ambiguity of the emotional side of love. The ambiguity lies in the fact that the emotion connected with human love originates in and is an expression of another basis of love, which is ontological. According to Paul Tillich,

> Love is an ontological concept. Its emotional element is a consequence of its ontological nature. It is false to define love by its emotional side. This leads necessarily to sentimental misinterpretation of the meaning of love and calls into question its symbolic application to the divine life. . . . The process of the divine life has the character of love. According to the ontological polarity of individual-

---

[18] *Ibid.*, p. 256.

ization and participation, every life-process unites a trend toward separation with a trend toward reunion. The unbroken unity of these two trends is the ontological nature of love. Its awareness as fulfillment of life is the emotional nature of love.[19]

Man's position as a loving being is somewhat analogous to that of any other living, animal structure in that all are to various degrees unaware of the ontological foundation of their basic drives. Teleological consciousness has never been implanted in lower animal life, and it exists only vaguely in man—only in those who have the intellectual courage to transcend the world of external relations to the level of ontological synthesis. Even though the language in practically every social discipline is laden with precepts of value, truth and goodness, only in a forceful ontology of being is there an open recognition that the reflection of such precepts in man's intellectual outlook is the natural expression of life as love. "Life," Tillich wrote, "is being in actuality and love is the moving power of life." [20] But human consciousness is not profoundly aware of love as the creative moments of being itself. It is aware of the impulse in terms of its more familiar signs. One kind of love expression which has come into prominence because of its quasi-scientific credibility is the *libido*, which is an expression of what is intensely personal in the love experience. A second form is love as *philia*, which is an outward thrust toward an equal, while a third is the eros experience of love in ascendancy. As Tillich expresses it,

> Love as *libido* is the movement of the needy toward that which fulfills the need. Love as *philia* is the movement of the equal toward union with the equal. Love as *eros* is the movement of that which is lower in power and meaning

[19] *Ibid.*, p. 279.
[20] Paul Tillich, *Love, Power and Justice* (London: Oxford University Press, 1954), p. 25.

to that which is higher. . . . But there is a form of love which transcends these, namely, the desire for fulfillment of the longing of the other being, the longing for his ultimate fulfillment. All love, except *agapé,* is dependent on contingent characteristics which change and are partial. . . . Agape is independent of these states. . . . *Agapé* unites the lover and the beloved because of the image of fulfillment which God has of both.[21]

The general function of love is to effect a union between separated beings, and the different forms of the love impulse express the various modes under which the person can react in a love situation. These do, in fact, reflect the stratified nature of human existence. On the one level there are man's biological or emotional urges striving toward a libido satisfaction; on another level there is man's consciousness of a subjective identity with others; on a third level there is man's spiritual urge to affirm himself in the utmost of spiritual creativity and perfection. In every case, however, the object of the impulse is that of the utmost realization of self; it is unavoidably egocentric, and insofar as the impulse is this alone it has no universal gravitational power. Taken in any of these ways the love impulse fulfills human nature, but does not unite it. It does not effect that kind of inner reunion which a whole society so urgently needs. It is the fourth kind of love, agapé, which unites the whole of mankind because it is able to transcend man in the flesh to the spiritual reality of man-in-the-world.

The totality of man-in-the-world unavoidably entails power, and power readily collectivizes in such a way that it incurs by compulsion what is ideally brought about by love. Power is a category which is appropriate to a collective but love is not. As power, the collective is *being* actualizing itself against the threat of another collective which is to the first a

---

21 Tillich, *Systematic Theology,* I, 280.

form of nonbeing. In either case, power is used by the collective to actualize itself, whether it relies on outright coercion or the most subtle forms of legal duress. But while power is assumed to function in a manner which is construed ideally to be that of love, love is nonetheless the foundation of power inasmuch as collective power is an expression of collective libido. The specific danger arises because the collective possesses no superior form of inner reality; it is utterly incapable of agapé in any form. It is for this reason, Tillich says, that justice intervenes in the social situation to effect the reconciliation which must be made through the instrument of power. "If justice," he wrote, "is the form of the reunion of the separated, it must include both the separation without which there is no love, and the reunion in which love is actualized." [22]

Where must one look to expose the higher expressions of the universality of human love? The philosophers of Greek antiquity were certainly aware of the transcending effects of the love impulse, and they tried to deal with these universally binding effects in a philosophical manner. But in Plato's *Symposium,* and in other works, the superior uniting function of the love impulse was never arrived at, mainly because the emphasis was placed on philosophical reason rather than on the meaning of agapé itself. For Plato especially, that which involved an irrational element, an element not completely expressible as reason, could not be wholly central in the concept of a universal good. The Greeks were certainly correct in exalting Reason as the ultimate reference of virtue, but they somehow failed to acknowledge that there is a reference for Reason which is being-itself, and that is being-itself which incites men to become binding agents between philosophy and action.

It is the action content of Christian love which closes the gap between philosophy and experience. What stands out especially is the existence-reality which it engenders. There is no

<hr>

[22] Tillich, *Love, Power and Justice,* p. 62.

contemporary "ism"—no identifiable strain of philosophy which can match its transforming power on experience; and even those who do not accept the divinity of Christ are touched by the Christian gospel of love and sacrifice. Christian love is incomprehensible to those who are unable to undergo it. That one can be drawn to carrying out a performance for which there is no recompense forthcoming seems to be an inane idea. The wondrous example which Dr. Albert Schweitzer set before the world was not for unusual skill in medicine or even for his dedication to it. It was the fact that he chose to forego a distinguished career involving music and philosophy, as well as medicine, in order to bring his healing art to people who could do little or nothing to repay him for his gift of health and life.

Only when the idea of mankind is explored in its full depth as a spiritual community does it become apparent that new compensatory sources must always be present to account for the natural desiccation of spiritual energy in man. It becomes apparent that only through the release of the creative spirituality in love and sacrifice that the human community becomes unified at all. Human consciousness with its open and buoyant spontaneity is responsible for most of the digressions from any real solidarity, and only through the possibility of an enormous centripetal binding force of love is it possible to overcome the centrifugal action of individual interest and pursuit. It is precisely in this regard that Christic energy achieves its full force and dimension. It achieves what pure obedience to the law fails to do—the release of the intuitive spirit in man to fulfill by his acts what the meaning of God's image in him is. These acts are not the result of sentimentality, nor the result of highly sophistical intellectual arguments. Just as the life impulse enters matter in its lowest, least complex and least stable forms, the love impulse works in the most uncomplicated of situations. It expresses itself through the only way open—the giving of oneself; of conveying, as Marcel would say, along with the gift, the presence of the giver.

Is the release of Christic energy a turning away from the world of fact? A rejection of the world of science? When science found its way into technology it was discovered that it had come this way without any set of moral aims. In this sense it could stand as something condemned. But science is more than just an accessory kind of activity. It was through science that man's consciousness awoke to the reality of the physical environment. That this should in some ways also incur a threat to what was held as man's true spirituality is what one would expect, for these have been no frontiers of exploration from which science has been barred. But while this may have aroused considerable concern about man's spiritual integrity as man, scientific discovery has come to a recognition of its own limitations. Even evolution, once sadly misinterpreted as a threat to man's position in the hierarchy of being, has lost most of its ominousness as a destroyer of man's most sacred beliefs. Even in his sinful state, man was the only creature touched directly by God to receive the gift of reason and a consciousness of Himself; and it was this idea which men wanted desperately to protect from any invasion of science. They believed that the theory of evolution automatically linked man with the lower world which they had come to despise as a kind of spiritual darkness. But mankind has somehow come to recognize the transparency of biological life to a higher order of transcendent spirituality, and of man's personal life to something even higher. Human life and consciousness may not be the final step in the scale of cosmic evolution, but instead a step pointing to the goal which this scale entails. "Man is not the center of the universe," Chardin wrote, "as once we thought in our simplicity, but something much more wonderful—the arrow pointing the way to the final unification of the world in terms of life." [23]

The limitations of philosophy alone now become apparent.

---

[23] Pierre Teilhard de Chardin, *The Phenomenon of Man* (New York: Harper & Brothers, 1951), p. 233.

Philosophy, the most sophisticated of all disciplines, maintains its intellectual hold, its lure for the restless spirit of inquiry. But philosophy alone does not satisfy the driving passion in man to be at one with the world; to unite with it by involving oneself organically with it at its highest level of spiritual reality. Plato's works, for example, point toward a resplendent ideal of Universal Reason to which man can aspire by pursuing the path toward true knowledge. But Plato did not make Universal Reason deeply personal and moving. As in so many other cases, philosophy here only points to the true and the real. It lacks the binding power to translate word into deed. Philosophy is indeed a contemplative experience in which one is momentarily removed from art, from science, from medicine, and from the work of the world. But it becomes truly vibrant when it is made *common;* when the one who experiences it is brought back into a living, pulsating world so that one can truly experience the fullness of what philosophy is.

Although the common philosophy, as it is conceived of here, is a glimpse of the eternal in the finite, of universal man embodied in the particular, there are some obstacles which block the advance of human consciousness toward its fullness of self-realization. The life of the spirit in man is that of his continually creating and recreating himself in the order of the infinite and the eternal. But through the medium of his own consciousness, man has only a refractory awareness of himself as a creative being. The difficulty arises because of the reluctance of consciousness in man to detach itself from the empirical world and to affirm itself in its own mode of being—freedom. Consciousness in man is spirit acknowledging itself to be real and to be present in the world. But it does not know itself in this same way as universal. Because consciousness is itself plastic to the numerous modalities in which the facts of the world are given, it is capable of scientific accuracy. Unfortunately, consciousness far too often takes this reflection of the natural world into itself as its highest capability, disregarding the fundamental inner freedom through which it exercises its own genius. To equate spirit as consciousness with the imminent processes of nature is a false ideal because these processes involve only the redistribution of existing matter and energy. Human creativity has no equivalence in organic life simply because it transcends in practically every case every organic life structure in which human consciousness occurs. It is a transition from the isolation and the limitation of static expression forms to the infinite and spiritual—a transition from the exoteric to the esoteric.

Because evolutionary development, even on the plane of historical occurrence, is an exoteric category, it cannot be regarded as the true manifestation of the growth of spirit in man. It is quite true that the work of civilization is the revelation of spirit in man, but civilization invariably entails its own materialization and mechanization which, Berdyaev says, "is precisely a process of disincarnation in which the historic embodiment of things is disappearing." [24] This disincarnation does not occur only in an outward sense of the social aspects of mankind. It penetrates into and shapes the consciousness of man himself. Like a machine which stamps out innumerable identical parts from a mass of metal, man takes on the mold of the disincarnated society in which he exists; he adopts the bourgeois image. As Berdyaev also writes,

> The scientist or the artist bears no likeness to the sage, the politician or the business man has certainly no resemblance to the knight. And all of them are blotted out by the image of the "bourgeois" which penetrates into each one of the professional types. The bourgeois is the completely socialized being, subordinate to *das man,* deprived of originality and of freedom of judgment and action.[25]

[24] Nicolas Berdyaev, *Freedom and the Spirit* (London: Geoffrey Bles: The Canterbury Press, 1935), p. 317.
[25] Berdyaev, *The Destiny of Man,* p. 243.

The most ambitious aim of the philosopher historian is to be able to see Spirit in man as finally and victoriously triumphant over the *das Man* figure in which the bourgeois element is always present. Hegel's *Phenomenology of the Spirit* and also his *Philosophy of History* are highly in accord with the idea that in a social dialectic the contradictions inherent with man's nature are evidently worked out in the advance of Spirit as Consciousness. The Marxian expectation was born out of the belief that social production, carrying forward the total sinfulness of mankind, would inevitably bring about that convulsive moment in history when all of the evil incumbent in social production would be expiated. Hegel's main configuration of history is that of the endless expansion of the consciousness of the Absolute. The Marxist synthesis of history has as its main focus an unending stretch of social peace and harmony commensurate with their moral demands. In both cases the goal of history overshadows the idea of a growing consciousness of mankind. In both cases there is posited a polarity of man's essential and his existential selves, and a reconciliation of these in time.[26] For a *common* philosophy, however, both positions are unacceptable. Recognizing the impossibility of reconciliation, it must nevertheless deal with conciliation. Realizing that redemption for infinity of that which is finite is an impossible ideal, it must nonetheless embrace the idea of the eternal redemption of mankind on earth.

The idea of redemption on earth, however, should not be construed as an eternal reconciliation of the Divine essence with something which has the permanent stain of evil attached

---

[26] In writing on the theme of reconciliation, Tillich says, "This belief is Hegel's basic error. . . . The world is not reconciled, either in the individual—as Kierkegaard shows—or in society—as Marx shows or in life as such—as Schopenhauer and Nietzsche show. Existence is estrangement and not reconciliation; it is dehumanization and not the expression of essential humanity." (Paul Tillich, *Systematic Theology*, Chicago: The University of Chicago Press, 1957, II, 25.)

to it. It is redemption which has to be understood in terms of the eternal creativity for which both man and the earth are the passive substances through which divine creativity is worked out. Because creativity in man is a multilayered phenomenon, as Tillich indicates by his several strata of the love impulse, redemption in this case is not a denial of the lower level but an affirmation of the higher. In other words, man's earthly redemption consists of the realization of his agapé potential rather than the negation of his libido.

The Christian expectation is founded on the creative nature of personality. Personality is a gracious radiation of being. It is the revelation of the Divine idea implanted in human spirituality. That is, spirituality is creativity; it is the continuous creation by that which is itself created. But while the redemptive task of creativity is the radical transformation of man by the Divine nature as personality, the marks of creativity also show man as overcoming the world. In other words, man overcomes the world by being himself overcome. As Berdyaev expressed it,

> The creative act is by its very nature ecstatic; it involves movement out beyond the boundaries; there is an act of transcendence in it. Creativeness is not an immanent process, nor susceptible of explanation in terms of immanence. There is always more in it than in any of the clauses by which it is sought to explain the creative power; . . . Creative activity will not come to terms with the given state of the world, it derives another.[27]

The concept of *person* is one which has drawn its content from a long period of man's evolutionary awakening. For a long, and culturally uneventful period, it was the world-in-man which determined the course of his routine existence. It

---

[27] Nicolas Berdyaev, *The Beginning and the End* (New York: Harper & Brothers, 1952), p. 174.

was a period in which the instinctive order of the lower world shaped human growth much as the earth supports and shapes the plant. From the upper Paleolithic period onward man-in-the world drew more and more away from a material direction of life close to the earth, and through tribal life and custom gradually formed and shaped a rule of law appropriate in a direct way to human life alone. But it was nonetheless, a law of the herd. It was a law appropriate to life in which the collective—the tribe—was the main reference. It was by this means that Judaism prepared for and carried out its mission as God's Chosen; as being the earthly means for carrying forward the truth of Yahweh's religion. For that matter, it is the ethics of law which sustains social and civic life even in the Christian community. But it is also an ethic which is negative; it preserves the life of the community while thwarting personal inventiveness and initiative. To be sure, the nature of life in the social collective—in even the most advanced forms of community—is such that the ethics of law must be applied. It is socially absurd to suppose that the security of the individual person ought to be subject to the prevailing spiritual condition of herd society. But what is a temporal necessity for the practical requirements of life in the collective ought not impose limitations on consciousness-in-general; on the life of the spirit in man. It is in this regard that the ethics of Grace replaces the ethics of law. The ethics of Grace is a reversal of the law of entropy in man. It is the force of renewal—of revitalization of the spiritual energy in man which makes ethics possible. Just as the earth requires every day a new amount of energy radiation from the sun in order to carry out its fecundating, creating role, the human community requires the constant infusion of the invigorating aspects of personality. Just as the figure of Christ typifies the new Logos—the New Being—so also is personality in man a logos in a lesser sense—it is the source of the meaning of life.

181

CHAPTER VI

The Uncommon: Nature as Mind

THE EVOLUTION OF MANKIND has taken millions of years. How long it took for a latent germ plasm to augment itself through one species generation after another into an erect *Pithecanthropus* one can now only guess. How far into the future this unfolding of latent human potential will extend is equally uncertain. But one point about which paleontologists, such as Chardin, are quite firm is that the growth of human consciousness is at present blatantly incomplete. Paleontological evidence—artifacts arranged in the order of a chronology of social development—suggests rather decisively that life structures tend to gravitate toward each other wherever there is a possibility of realizing a greater life whole. Cellular structures have internally the same type of organic composition, whether they exist singly or as metazoa. Metazoan particles do not originate by a chance clustering of single cells, but rather by a reproductive process in which cellular division is carried out in accordance with the requirements of a higher unifying structure. Individual cells which comprise metazoa are not less complete in terms of existential perfection than single ones, but their independence of function is curtailed in order that there may be realized the higher type of reality which the multicellular organism achieves. It is from such biological evidence that the higher laws of nature become apparent. One of these is that coexistence is a basic condition for evolutionary development. Coexistence is the means by which nature, transforming itself by becoming inwardly social, achieves new levels of creativity.

The main reason for supposing that the growth of human consciousness is not yet complete is that consciousness, while admitting the presence of higher laws within itself, is far from able, in a universal sense, to acknowledge these laws as binding on itself. Although mankind accepts—even welcomes—social coexistence, it does so only by creating a superior kind of social reality which is able to enforce the laws of the whole upon the individual man. That is, man has so far been able to recognize himself in his social context only through recognizing also what he is able and free to do by himself as opposed to what he must be forced to do in order that the social community shall survive. The popular appeal of democracy as a method of government lies in its greater humanization than any other political method. There is always a certain pressure of egocenteredness within a person which makes him reluctant to accept the idea of a higher reality of a social whole transcending his own privately conceived existence. But in political situations where a social decision is required, the same person is usually willing to assent to the expression of the majority; perhaps because of his recognizing that the will of the majority is itself a larger instance of egocentered decisions.

The ideas of the individual and the majority apply, however, only in a very narrow sense to man's existential situation. These apply to the social condition because of man's sensitivity to ideas of equality. The right which accrues to a majority simply because it is greater in number than a minority conceals another right attributed to it out of individual interest —that of being the instrument of distributive justice. Distributive justice is concerned with the equitable apportionment of whatever form of social good a government is able to implement; it is concerned with the universal application of the law. The idea of equality seems to be the overriding social concern of man's psychic consciousness. Accordingly, this observation is not a criticism but an acknowledgment of the depth to which human consciousness explores itself and the extent to which it builds for itself a set of social realities which reflect its own value designations. It is in this sense that philosophy, constructed out of the modes of man's self-affirmation, becomes *common*. That is, it is common to man.

The common philosophy, however, is by no means a complete account, or even an attempt to make a complete accounting, of existential reality. Man participates in the life process, but life is itself transcendent. It is an outcome of a cosmic continuum which has endured for billions of years, and it stretches back in time to a temporal oblivion about which man can now only guess. The point is that human consciousness arose at a very late hour in the world's evolutionary story and that it is the result of a cosmic guiding field which, in its existential embrace of forms of life, is most uncommon. It is an absolute which is entirely originary.

While the *common* in philosophy is that which can be shared through endless multiplication, the *uncommon* is that whose being is eternal and that neither multiplies nor divides itself in any way. Although any purported description by practical terminology is unavoidably a halting one, the concept which shall denote the uncommon is *Mind*. The term is used as the most proper analogue of man's relation to nature because it denotes consciousness in its entire structural reality rather than as something which is a finite reflection of itself— such as consciousness in man. The cosmic milieu in which Mind has made itself incarnate as the living world is Nature. But Nature does not consist merely of the living vestiges of the creative process which are available momentarily to man and are at his disposal. In its most genuine sense, nature is that totality of creative impulses which Mind has bestowed upon the earth. Nature is thus not just the power of earthly creation; it is also the power of critical inner transformation. It is in this sense that Nature generated numerous steps of life transformations which graduated, one out of another, and culminated in a finite deployment of mind as human consciousness and knowing.

Although the minded organism which is man has made enormous progress in bringing so much of the cosmic milieu and man's geological milieu within the reach of his understanding, the limits of mind in man have not only slowed but may also have retarded his own progress of self-illumination. While the rise of analytic intellectualism greatly increased man's grasp of what is physically present and at hand, it also tended to distort his inner sense of what is ultimately most real. When man lived largely through the efforts of his intuitive consciousness, he was also perhaps quite certain of his own surmisings. Only through reflective intelligence—only when mind began to demand that it become empirically confirmed in order to be satisfied—did the fact of doubt or uncertainty occur.

The task here, however, is a concern with Universal Mind as a pervasive totality. The inquiry must begin with what is most ostensibly given, and this is not Universal Mind nor mind in the ordinary sense, but what is given in sensation— matter or the material world. In this original act of cognition, the two ways in which Universal Mind are externalized in man find their equivalence in two corresponding ways of apprehension. That is, through sensation—which is a Universal Mind product of mind-body synthesis—one encounters the bare fact of matter in space through sensory apprehension. Through the organizing and reflective power of man's own mind, one realizes that there is not just matter but matter existing under a recognizable structural organization. It is this original act of human knowing which opens to man the pervasive aspect of nature as mind in the whole cosmic milieu. John Boodin pointed out that

> Mind has its permanent claim, and matter has its permanent claim to reality within the whole, and neither exists in isolation. While mind is higher in the scale and therefore more valuable, it is not more real than matter, nor is it more necessary than matter to the economy of the whole. Mind requires the organization of matter for its realization as much as matter of a lower order requires mind for its guidance, and both are aspects of the hierarchical organization of the cosmos.[1]

Aside from the mutual interdependence of mind and matter in nature, there is also the polarization of these in the entire medium of cosmic creativity. The polarization does not entail the necessity of matter having been present for an eternity, for the polarization is not that of opposites in a qualitatively equal sense, but rather that of a creative source acting upon that which has been created. Boodin points out that had there been no cosmic guiding field there would have been no evolution, and, conversely, had there been no reacting matter there would not have been evolution either. Evolution presupposes matter in the condition of becoming, including the bare coming-to-be of matter in itself, apart from any formal determination. Plotinus regarded matter as owing its form—that essential being implanted in it—to the creative effect of light as energy. That which is totally matter-in-itself is that in which this creative power has never entered; it is that which shades off into total darkness. It is that in which there is no formal being present, and, while this is impossible

---

[1] John Elof Boodin, *Cosmic Evolution* (New York: The Macmillan Company, 1925), p. 128.

for the human mind to conceive, it also indicates the possibility of an appearance point of matter as an inertial subject. That is, as an inertial subject it is completely passive to the transforming power of a cosmic guiding field.

The polarization of mind and matter in nature is one of function rather than of position. Matter, for example, has no power of cancelling out mind. On the contrary, matter is the universal instrument through which universal mind particularizes itself. Every *body* is an incorporation of mind in matter; and in terms of its finite forms of structural determination, being is endlessly multiplied. That is, a tiny particle by comparison with more highly complex structures appears to be of minimal structural significance and bears the mark of mind in its organizational principle. The work of nature is the progressive embodiment of mind in particle behavior; and the work of evolution is that of a gradual but also a more thorough implementation of more of mind's detail in living structures. Evolution does not occur in reverse. It does not occur by stripping species structures of their more advanced details. Evolution consistently entails an increase in structural "complexification" or, in simpler language, an increase in being.

Another thing which should be noted regarding evolution is that there is no steady unbroken ascent in any case. Chardin notes that since man's arrival evolutionary pressure toward biological development has noticeably dropped. The instinctive reflexes which now condition animal and insect behavior were no doubt themselves the outcome of an elongated process of inner development, but with the development of these reflexes toward their full operative level, evolutionary pressure has dropped off noticeably in that direction as well. The phenomenon of cosmic evolution is one of a series of graduated performance levels of numerous strata of finite being, each one operating dependently on less complex material structures, as the protoplasm in a cell depends on protein molecules, and each in turn acts as a support for more complex substances in the hierarchy of being. The polarity as it is operative in nature is most truly represented in man—in the existential coalition of matter-in-itself entering into the digestive process of converting molecular energy into cell energy, and of mind in its supreme function of intuitive and reflective intelligence. While evolutionary processes take place within tiny, even infinitesimal, areas of geological activity, the unifying aspect of the process as a whole takes place under the direction of the cosmic guiding field. The reason that the process may seem so slow that it is imperceptible to human knowing is that human knowing and consciousness are a part of the total process. It took billions of years just for the growth and hardening of personhood to occur, and by far the greater portion of that time was given over to the original period of the growth of animal protoplasm. It was in animal protoplasm that the germ plasm of the hominoid species was kept alive until that time when the germ plasm itself took over animal protoplasm in order to work out its own evolutionary design.

Although the main concern in the study of historic evolution has been that of discovering lines of progressive ascent toward higher levels of internal organization and cosmic adaptation, the entire phenomena of cosmic and geological evolution are processes of separate lineal patterns running parallel to one another, intersecting one another, and perhaps also overtaking one another. It is true that evolutionary pressure has dropped off in a considerable number of cases involving both plants and animals. It is also true that some species have disappeared. It is a rational temptation to suppose that this retarding of the evolutionary process automatically imposes corresponding limits upon the evolutionary possibilities of higher species for which the lower ones are a support. However, it is just as plausible to suppose that certain species drop out because they are no longer necessary in the whole economy of nature; and the fact that developmental processes have frozen in some forms of lower animal and insect life may be because their usefulness in the economy of nature had reached its limit. At any rate, the range of possibilities for any one stratum does not depend entirely on the support potential of that from which it derives its energy. Human bodies, for example, do not produce minds in accordance with the existential perfection of the human torso, for mind is a special kind of perfection indigenous only to minds. It is certainly true that without an adequate body a mind does not function, and it is also true that impairment of the function of man's physical self has a direct effect on his mental faculties. However, in spite of this dependence, mind in man has an autonomous function which is not a derivative of some physiological condition. Mind, for example, is not identical with the neural structure of the cerebrum; it is the organizational principle of the brain, and also its animating instrument.

Another matter which ought to be of utmost concern for the student of evolution is that evolution does not necessarily achieve its prime significance solely in the idea of ascent. What is also especially important is the types and grades of interaction which occur and what these mean when related to the most common form of interaction—human communication. Although human communication is carried on by sound waves, which are really waves of air, and by light waves, which are the radiant energy waves of a luminous body—it is the receptor end of communication which is the most baffling. With some understanding of wave energy phenomena one can grasp the idea of retinal surfaces being agitated to produce electrostatic signals, and one can also understand how these signals act as emissaries to the brain where their energy is then transformed into the energy of sight recognition. But what is beyond human comprehension is the process by which the receptor organs were first formed. It is quite certain that it was the cosmic source of solar wave energy which aroused the responsiveness of matter to assemble as protoplasmic structures, but the direction of the response could only have come from the guidance of the cosmic field itself. The concept of cosmic guidance must be understood in terms of a unifying influence implicit in the energy of the field. It is equally as important, however, to recognize that there were different kinds of responses on different strata levels of particle behavior, and that the evolutionary process could not by-pass or cut short the achievement of these higher strata levels. Protoplasm, for example, is capable of a kind of response which mineral particles are not. Also, it is quite apparent that there are several basic types of matter in which natural processes are operative. There is, first of all, inorganic matter —matter which has no life quality attached to it. There is also protoplasm, having performance possibilities of internal organization and of aggregation far in excess of the inorganic. Above protoplasm in the hierarchy of performance potential there is minded matter—matter in which the quality of self-awareness has been achieved and in which also the psychic reality incumbent within the individual achieves the existential focus of ego-centeredness. Awareness of one's self as a *self* is a high mark of evolutionary achievement. But for this to be achieved, there must be that self-convergence in psychic activity which actualizes for itself an awareness focus. This can only be brought about by that which is itself eternally creative. According to Boodin,

> If there is a nisus toward divinity, it is because divinity, the supreme organization of harmony, beauty, goodness, and love, is active throughout the cosmos, stimulating the evolution of every part of the direction of divinity. As light stimulates toward the adaptation of seeing light,

so divinity stimulates toward communion with itself. Light beats upon our earth-born beings, and permeates them, that it may stimulate in them the organization to see light; life beats upon them to awaken them to receive life; thought acts to create the response to creative thought.[2]

There is no verbal symbol which is a denotational equivalent of the directive activity of Mind in the production of emergent species. From man's own level of awareness he can look toward cosmic creativity as some kind of radiant consciousness. But this is something involving much more than wave energy transmission. Not only is life itself centered in each living unity; the various organs with which the units are equipped to carry out their total functions are themselves highly adapted to carrying out their respective roles. The ear prepares in water for hearing in air, and the eye prepares in the dark for seeing in the light. In each case the actualizing process is carried out in the appropriate period when the whole organism prepares for birth. While there are separate centered foci for organ production, there is also a focus of the whole which is contained in the fertilized cell which is the origin of the reproductive process.

The phenomenon of centered activity is a highly pervasive one in all organic activity. In fact, it is the persistent tendency toward realizing an existential focus which is so highly characteristic of mind, and this occurs on several existential strata. Boodin points out that

> The milieu of mind is threefold. There is the inner complexity—the interpenetration of systems within any one mental organization—a complexity which surpasses vastly that of the organism which is included within the higher

---

[2] *Ibid.*, p. 123.

unity. There is, further, the social milieu, the relation of mind to other minds, the intersubjective continuum. There is, finally, the milieu of nature of which mind and society are part and within which they have been evolved.[3]

Among the numerous strata of being which have arisen and have become distinct from one another, the one which exists within the milieu of mind and mind—social interaction —is the one which has incurred the greatest amount of internal contradiction. The fact of mankind's self-inflicted devastation tends to arouse the feeling that human freedom was a cosmic mistake; that mankind would have been much better integrated, socially, had his social responses been due to a set of instinctive reflexes rather than to his own open choice. But every such view is conditioned by the perspective which the person has himself achieved—a perspective which represents but a fragment of a total social outlook. That human freedom has incurred the possibility of widespread and intense tribulation is certainly true. It is also true that the valuation of human freedom is done through the act of freedom—which means also that the person doing the evaluation is free to choose his own criteria. Human freedom is not only a social condition; it is also a cosmic fact. It is a fact which entailed a long developmental period of evolutionary activity within an enormous cosmic envelope, and it would be a mistake to assume that it is everywhere perfectly developed. It was, first of all, the necessary condition for the expansion of human consciousness and a corresponding rise in intellectual achievement. This took place at a much faster rate than the biological transformation which produced man as the hominoid species. In other words, much less time elapsed between Pithecanthropus and Newton than that which produced Pithecanthropus as an erect user of tools. If human society is imperfectly or-

---

[3] *Ibid.*, p. 200.

ganized, it is not as if man is incapable of ultimately achieving a society which is more perfectly centered and internally ordered. Social evolution is at this time far from complete. It is possible to make this assertion, at least as a plausible position, because of popular recognition of ideal conditions not yet achieved. Also, while man may not now be disposed to cross over to a higher level of social achievement, he can at least look backward and mark what are the real instances of historical growth. The emergence of multicellular organisms was a new kind of creative reality which took place in time. It took place because of single cellular bodies and maintained a potential for larger forms of organization. The emergence of biological life on the level of metazoa was a new step in the exploratory advance of nature as mind. This was accomplished through reaching a new synthesis of dynamic equilibrium whereby the life energy present in each cellular particle was brought into a new focus of biological orientation—the law of the whole. It was also the gradual realization of the law of the whole which marked the physiological evolution of the hominoid species. But man's social development occurs through a far different course. The whole in this case is not a suprabeing whose concrete expression requires some decrease in being on the part of its members. On the contrary, the whole in this case is not one of parts but of things which are whole in themselves and increase their wholeness of being through the other. In its incarnation as human mind, Nature as Mind achieved its highest level of creative synthesis while using matter as its creative base. But the new level of synthesis became also a new base, and from here the old processes of division and partition which are characteristic of material creativity no longer apply. Human social evolution is the life of the spirit of man. It shares with material evolution the fact that its downward turn and its upward turn in creativity occur simultaneously. Social evolution is not marked by any

193

high level precision of organic function, but rather by the level of social interaction in living protoplasm which is carried out through the release and the gaining of energy units among molecular bodies. Mind on the level of sociality is an entirely different energy system. It depends on visual and vocal apparatuses which are highly complex perceptive organs. The life of the spirit in man, however, depends in a far greater sense on materials which are characteristic of spirit itself; on innumerable meanings and shades of meanings, on various types and degrees of feeling, all of which continue to arouse new creative concepts and symbolic expression forms in an uninterrupted stream. The buoyant spontaneity of mind at the level of human reflective thought is due to its being less bound by the inertia of matter, and it exists, therefore, in its most truly creative fashion. But it can become stifled even here by an excessive ego concern when the focus of consciousness becomes clouded by materialistic considerations. The ego in itself is that whose nature is to be free, to be unbound by the gravity of matter in order to be truly creative. It is through his freedom that man leaves his impress upon the world in the form of human culture; in the continual work of synthesis of new personal achievements which also then continually reshape man in his social dimension.